E S T A T E   P U B L I C A T I O N S

·XETER · EXMOUTH

·UDLEIGH SALTERTON · EXMINSTER · WEST

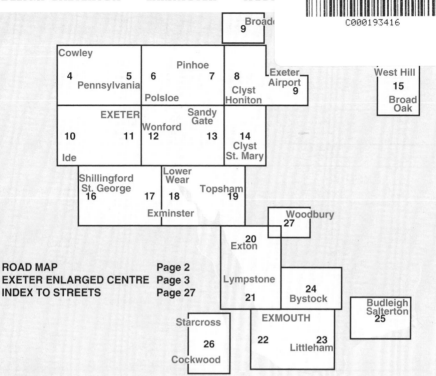

Broad... 9
Cowley
4 5 Pennsylvania
6 Pinhoe 7 Polsloe
8 Clyst Honiton
Exeter Airport 9
West Hill 15 Broad Oak
EXETER 10 11 Ide
Wonford 12 Sandy Gate 13
14 Clyst St. Mary
Shillingford St. George 16 17
Lower Wear 18 Topsham 19 Exminster
Woodbury 27
20 Exton
Lympstone 21
24 Bystock
Budleigh Salterton 25
Starcross 26 Cockwood
EXMOUTH 22 23 Littleham

ROAD MAP Page 2
EXETER ENLARGED CENTRE Page 3
INDEX TO STREETS Page 27

Scale of street plans: 4 Inches to 1 Mile (unless otherwise stated)

Motorway
'A' Road / Dual
'B' Road / Dual
Minor Road / Dual
Track
Pedestrianized
Railway / Station
Footpath

Every effort has been made to verify the accuracy of information in this book but the publishers cannot accept responsibility for expense or loss caused by an error or omission. Information that will be of assistance to the user of the maps will be welcomed.

The representation on these maps of a road, track or path is no evidence of the existence of a right of way.

Stream / River

Canal
One-way Street
Car Park
Public Convenience
Tourist Information
Place of Worship
Post Office

Street plans prepared and published by ESTATE PUBLICATIONS, Bridewell House, TENTERDEN, KENT.
The Publishers acknowledge the co-operation of the local authorities of towns represented in this atlas.

Ordnance Survey® This product includes mapping data licensed from Ordnance Survey® with the permission of the Controller of Her Majesty's Stationery Office.

Estate Publications 361 G

ISBN 1 84192 201 3

Cheriton Fitzpaine
Cadbury
A3072
Upton Hellions
Stockleigh Pomeroy
Sandford
Up Exe
A396
Bradninch
Colebrook
Mutterton
Dulford
Westcott
Norman's Green
Langford
Plymtree
Silverton
Hele
Clyst Hydon
Thorverton
Shobrooke
Shute
R. Exe
Rewe
Clyst St. Lawrence
Higher Tale
Crediton
R. Yeo
Nether Exe
Budlake
Talaton
Brampford Speke
R. Culm
Westwood
R. Clyst
Uton
Hookway
M5
B3181
Whimple
Newton St Cyres
Stoke Canon
Upton Pyne
Broadclyst
A377
A30
Fairmile
Poltimore
Cowley
Dog Village
Tedburn St Mary
Pinhoe
B3174
Exeter
Rockbeare
Whipton
Clyst Honiton
West Hill
Pathfinder Village
Whitestone
29
B3212
Marsh Green
Broad Oak
Sowton
A30
S
EXETER SERVICES
Clyst St. Mary
Longdown
B3212
Aylesbeare
Farringdon
Venn Ottery
A3015
30
A3052
Ide
Alphington
Topsham
Clyst St. George
Woodbury Salterton
Shillingford St George
B3193
A379
A30
B3179
Woodbury
Hawkerland
B 3178
31
Dunchideock
Ebford
B3180
Exminster
A379
A376
Doddiscombsleigh
Kennford
Exton
Yettington
S
Christow
Higher Ashton
KENNFORD SERVICES
Kenn
R. Kenn
Powderham
Lympstone
East Budleigh
R. Otter
Lower Ashton
Kenton
Tottiford Resr.
Trusham
A38
A380
R. EXE
Starcross
B3178
Littleham
Hennock
Cockwood
Budleigh Salter
Bovey Tracey
B3193
B3344
Ashcombe
Exmouth
Chudleigh
B3192
A379
Chudleigh Knighton
Dawlish Warren
Ideford
Heathfield
Luton
Dawlish
B3193
A382
A38
Preston
Holcombe
Teigngrace
Bishopsteignton
Kingsteignton
A381
Newton Abbot
Teignmouth
River Teign
Shaldon
Netherton
Combeinteignhead
West Ogwell
Haccombe
Stokeinteignhead
A380
East Ogwell
Babbacombe Bay
Coffinswell
Denbury
Abbotskerswell
Maidencombe
Ipplepen
Kingskerswell
Barton
A379

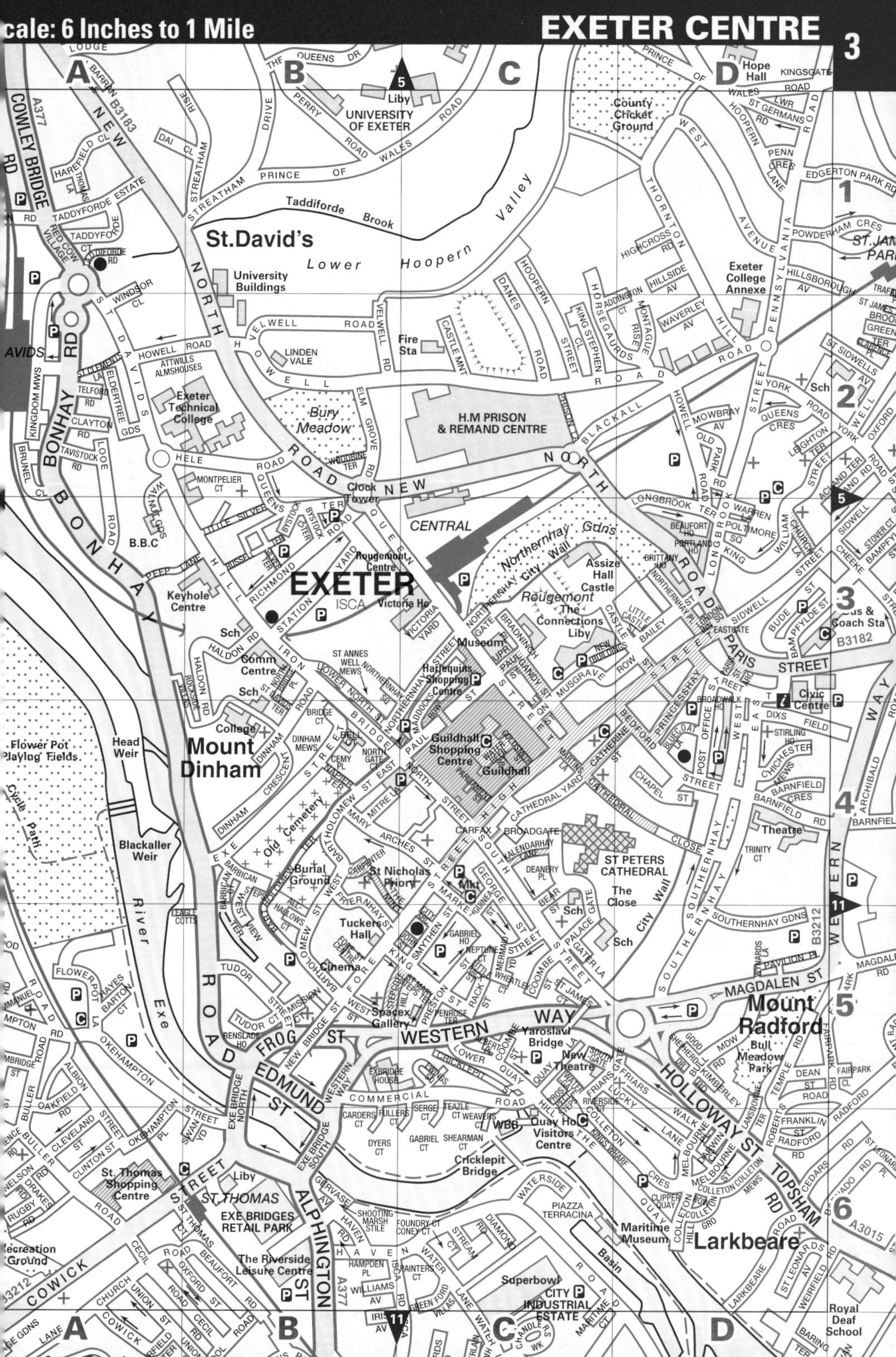
St.David's
Lower Hoopern Valley
Taddiforde Brook
UNIVERSITY OF EXETER
Liby
County Cricket Ground
Hope Hall
Exeter College Annexe
University Buildings
Exeter Technical College
ATTWILLS ALMSHOUSES
Bury Meadow
H.M PRISON & REMAND CENTRE
Fire Sta
LINDEN VALE
Clock Tower
CENTRAL
Northernhay Gdns
City Wall
Assize Hall
Castle
Rougemont
The Connections Liby
Rougemont Centre
EXETER
ISCA
Victoria Ho
B.B.C
Keyhole Centre
Comm Centre
Museum
Harlequins Shopping Centre
Guildhall Shopping Centre
Guildhall
Mount Dinham
College
Head Weir
Flower Pot Playing Fields
Cycle Path
Blackaller Weir
River Exe
Old Cemetery
Burial Ground
St Nicholas Priory
Tuckers Hall
Cinema
Mkt
ST PETERS CATHEDRAL
The Close
City Wall
Sch
Civic Centre
Bus & Coach Sta
Theatre
Spacex Gallery
WESTERN WAY
FROG ST
EDMUND ST
Yaroslavl Bridge
New Theatre
Quay Ho Visitors Centre
Cricklepit Bridge
Mount Radford
Bull Meadow Park
HOLLOWAY ST
TOPSHAM RD
Larkbeare
Maritime Museum
Basin
Superbowl
CITY INDUSTRIAL ESTATE
PIAZZA TERRACINA
St. Thomas Shopping Centre
ST THOMAS
EXE BRIDGES RETAIL PARK
The Riverside Leisure Centre
ALPHINGTON ST
Recreation Ground
COWICK ST
Royal Deaf School
NEW NORTH ROAD
BONHAY RD
COWLEY BRIDGE RD
PRINCE OF WALES ROAD
STREATHAM RISE
QUEENS DR
HOWELL ROAD
BLACKALL ROAD
PENNSYLVANIA ROAD
SIDWELL STREET
PARIS STREET
HIGH STREET
SOUTHERNHAY
MAGDALEN ST
COMMERCIAL ROAD
OKEHAMPTON STREET
A377
B3183
B3182
B3212
A3015

COWLEY

Cowley

Exwick

Nadderwater

Foxhayes

A B C D

Hill Close Copse

Higher Park Plantation

Hidden Valley

Cowley Bridge

Weir

Exwick Wood

Exwick Barton

Bolsters Wood

The Knap

Exwick Leat

Exwick Mills

Exwick Middle School

Foxhayes First School

Superstore

Attwells Farm

Whitestone Cross

Barley Wood

Cleve House

Exwick Valley Villas

Health Centre

Thomas H

Cowley Mede

Exwick Playing Field

Civil Service Sports Grnd

Cemetery

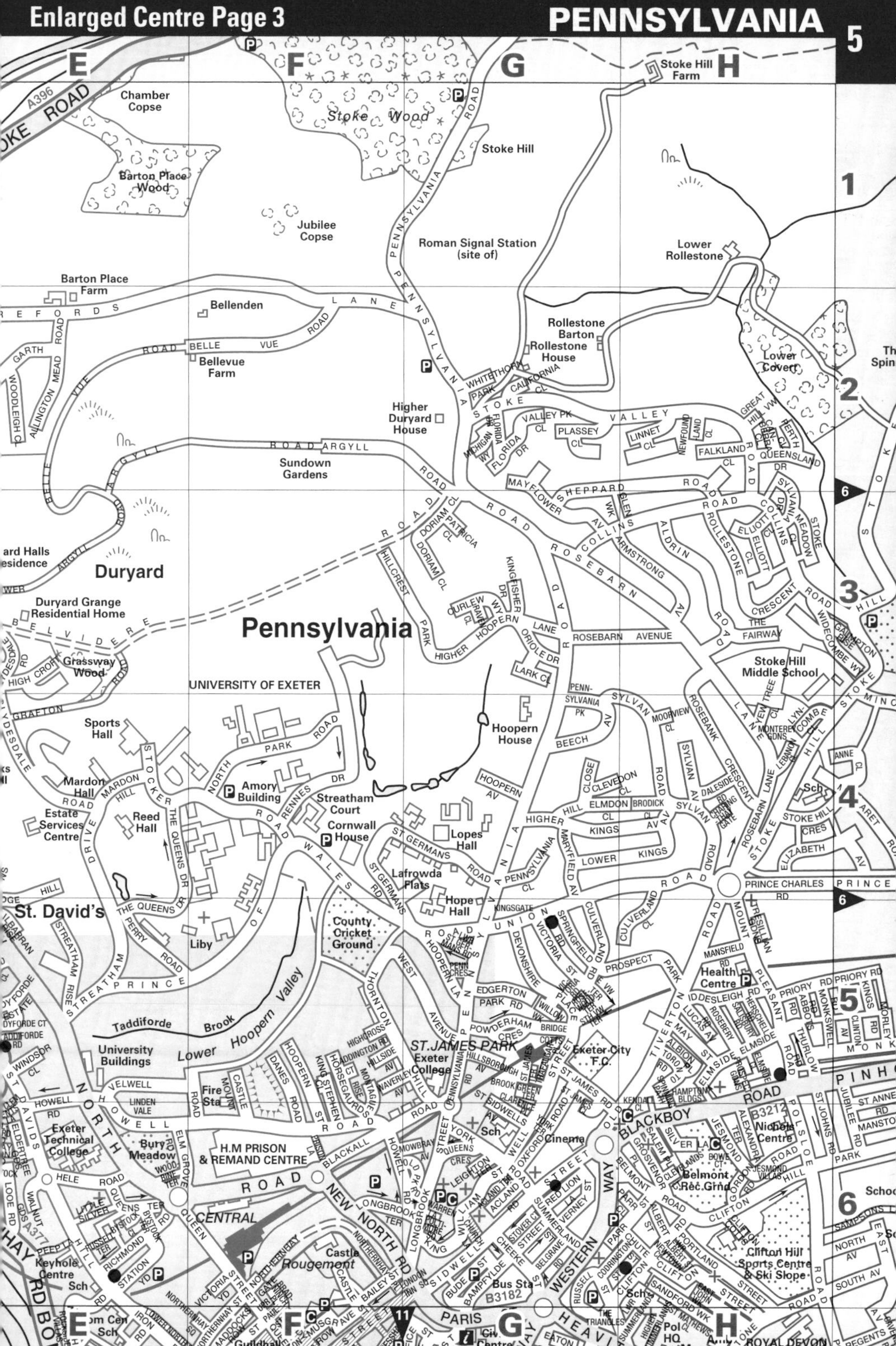

E   F   G   H

Stoke Hill Farm

Chamber Copse

Stoke Wood

Stoke Hill

Barton Place Wood

Jubilee Copse

Roman Signal Station (site of)

Lower Rollestone

Barton Place Farm

Bellenden

Lower Covert

The Spin

BELLE VUE

Bellevue Farm

Rollestone Barton Rollestone House

WHITETHORN

Higher Duryard House

Sundown Gardens

VALLEY PK

PLASSEY

LINNET

Falkland

Queensland

Duryard

Duryard Grange Residential Home

Grassway Wood

Pennsylvania

ROSEBARN AVENUE

Stoke Hill Middle School

THE FAIRWAY

UNIVERSITY OF EXETER

Hoopern House

Sports Hall

Mardon Hall

Amory Building

Streatham Court

Cornwall House

Lopes Hall

ELMDON

BRODICK

KINGS

Estate Services Centre

Reed Hall

Lafrowda Flats

Hope Hall

St. David's

Liby

County Cricket Ground

PRINCE CHARLES RD

Health Centre

University Buildings

Lower Hoopern Valley

St. JAMES PARK

Exeter College

Exeter City F.C.

Taddiforde Brook

Fire Sta

BLACKBOY

Belmont Rec. Grnd

Exeter Technical College

Bury Meadow

H.M PRISON & REMAND CENTRE

Cinema

Keyhole Centre Sch

CENTRAL

Castle Rougemont

Bus Sta

Clifton Hill Sports Centre & Ski Slope

Guildhall

Paris

ROYAL DEVON

Stoke Hill Farm

Grid references (top): A, B, C, D
Grid references (side): 1, 2, 3, 4, 5, 6

Pin Brook · Five Oaks · Rixdale · The Cottage · Hilltop · CHEYNEGATE · CHURCH · The Spinney · HILL · STOKE · MILE · HEATH BROOK MEWS · HEATH · HARRINGTON · HEATHBARTON · LANE

Stoke Hill · Mincinglake Valley Park · Mincinglake Stream · CELIA CRESCENT · COTTEY CRES · CHANCELLORS · SAVOY HILL · IOLANTHE · PENDRAGON RD · GARETH · TINTAGEL · AVALON · TRISTAN CL · ELAINE CL · KING GDNS · MILE GDNS · MERLIN · PERCIVALE · GALAHAD CL · CAMELOT · MOORED CL · LANCELOT · PELLINORE · ARTHURS · PINWOOD · JUNIPER · SPRUCE CL · WHITE BEAM · ILEX · FOX ROAD · TAMARISK · MEDLAR LA · BROOKSIDE CL · CENTRAL CRES · ARENA PARK · BEACON LANE · DRIVE · WAY · SUMMER · Eastern Field · Exeter Arena Athletics Stadium

St. James High School & Sports Centre · Beacon Heath First School · School · GUINEVERE · EXCALIBUR · FOURACRE CL · ATKINSON · ROUND TABLE · WOODBURY · BETTYSMEAD · CRESCENT · MILE LANE · BEACON LANE · EDMONTON RD · ST KATHERINES RD · CALTHORPE · PHILIP · ALBERT · LATIMER RD · UPLANDS DR · BRIDESPRING · MARYPOLE RD · WYNFORD RD · WK · ANNE CL · MARGARET CL · MINCINGLAKE ROAD · WIDECOMBE WY · CHARLTON · STOKE HILL · ST ELIZABETH ROAD · STOKE HILL CRES · LEBANON · TERLINGS · CRESWELL CRES · GREENSLAND · SYLVAN MEADOW · DRS LANE

Bettysmead Playing Field · Depot · PRINCE CHARLES ROAD · BETTYSMEAD CT · BENNETT SQ · WIDGERY RD · KENNERLEY AV · WOOLSERY AV · AVENUE · VILLAGE · WHIPTON · WESTBROOK CL · PRIESTLEY AV · KINGSLEY AV · WALLACE RD · SUWALLACE · THE MEDE · THE MEDE · SUMMERWAY · Summerway Middle School · ORWELL CL · GARTH · BERN · ADETTE CL · WALPOLE CL · MERWAY · MASEFIELD RD · SHERIDAN RD · AUSTEN · HACKERAY · THACKERAY · SUMMERWA · ROYSTO

Polsloe Priory · Works · PRIORY RD · KINGS · ABBOTS RD · ELTON · CLINTON · TUFFERY RD · DEVON RD · SWELL · CLOISTER RD · CLIFFORD RD · BEACON AV · BEACON AVENUE · BEACON · WIDGERY RD · POLSLOE BRIDGE · Honeylands School · LAMACRAFT · BRANCH HO · FLAYES ALMSHOUSES · Whipton · Schools · HILL · BROOKWAY · CRESCENT · LLOYDS · LYFIELD · BARTON · DURHAM · WHIP HOSP

PINHOE ROAD · MONKS RD · THURLOW · JUBILEE RD · ST ANNES RD · ST MARKS · COMMINS RD · MANSTON RD · FOWEY · WYKES · HERBERT RD · PAMELA RD · TARBET · FULFORD · THOMPSON RD · HAMLIN LANE · HAMLIN LANE ROAD · THE PINNEY · STADDON LANE · BONVILLE · CLIFFORD · ALLER · THORNPARK · POLSLOE HILL · ST JOHNS RD · LADYSMITH RD · PARK · School · Schools · SAMPSONS LA · PRETORIA RD · NORTH AV · EAST AV · SOUTH AV · HANOVER ROAD · LOWER AV · THIRD AV · Higher Cemetery · Hamlin Lane Playing Field · HAMLIN GDNS · SWEETBRIER · DAWN CL · CARLYON GDNS · CARLYON CL · MADISON CL · WAYSIDE · GEORGES RD · BROWNING · CRES · WAUGHAN · BODLEY RD · HEATHER · HEADLAND LA · HEADLAND CRES · MULBERRY · THORNPARK RISE · BLACKTHORN CRES · THORN · RISE · RUSSELL · PIPPIN · DURHAM · LEYPARK CRES

WYNDHAM · NTH LAWN RD · CHARD ROAD · WHIPTON LANE · ALFRED RD · VAUGHAN · REGENTS · NORMANDY RD · ART RD · 12

AL DEVON

E
F
G
H
1
2
3
4
5
6
Park Farm
Withy Bridge
Moonhill Copse
Ash Copse
Old Park Farm
West Clyst Farm
Woolsgrove Farm
Home Farm
Pinn Court Farm
Pinhoe
Pinhoe St Michaels School
Warehouse
PINHOE TRADING ESTATE
Clinic
Station Road Playing Field
Albany Farm
Brookhayes Childrens Home
Monkerton
Superstore
Gipsy Hill Hotel
Pinhoe House
GIPSY HILL MEWS
Redhayes
Ellen Tinkham School
Tilbury Douglas House
Depot
THE EXETER BUSINESS PARK
DIY Superstore
Gemini Radio
Hotel
Park & Ride
Sowton Brake
M5 JUNCTION 29
M5
A30
B3181
CLYST HILL WEST ROAD
PINN HILL ROAD
MAIN ROAD
HONITON ROAD
HONITON RD
PINHOE

A   B   C   D

1
Kerswell
Barton
Brockhill
Wishford
Farm
HELLINGS
PARK LANE
STATION
TRADING
ESTATE
Clyst
Valley

Clyst
m
LANE
MOSSHAYNE
2
LANE
HUNGRY FOX
ESTATE
Shermoor
Farm
COTTERELL RD
7
Mosshayne
SHERCROFT CL
ROA
3
MOSSHAYNE
Works

MILL
TITHEBARN LANE
LANE
Hayes
Farm
ROAD
4

ANE
LANE
7
WATERSLADE LANE
CLYSTHONITON
LANE
SHIP LANE
ST MICHAELS CL
ST MICHAELS
ST HILL
5
BLACKHORSE
ENDSLEIGH CRES
Clyst Honiton
Bridge
Clyst
Honiton
CHURCH SIDE
Sch
LA
HONITON RD
H
A30
Home
Farm
B3184
ROAD
SOWTON LANE
6
Marlborough
Farm
Sowton
Brake
SOWTON
A   B   14   C   D

A B C D

1

Broadclyst

Clyston Mill

B3181

QUEENS SQ

SCHOOL LA

Sch

CHURCH CL

TOWN HILL

HELLINGS GDNS

BURROW

ROAD

BURROW

ROAD

CHURCH LA

WILTSHIER CL

SUNNYFIELD

SMALL LA

GRACEY CT

HOLLY CL

Rec Grnd

WILLOW GDNS

WOODLAND

BROAD VW

WOODLAND RD

POUNDSLAND

MAPLE ROAD

SYCAMORE CL

ELM CLOSE

ACLAND RD

MWS

TREE VW

GREEN TREE

ROAD

Crabhayes

2

Paynes Farm

River Clyst

Jarvishayes

OLD COACH RD

SANDERS CL

ORCHARD GDNS

Dog Village

STATION ROAD

WOODBURY VW

TOWER

Clyst Vale Community College

ROAD

SANDY

3

B3181

4

Exeter Airport

5

BUSINESS PARK

INDUSTRIAL ESTATE

OAK

FAIR

CLOSE

EXETER AIRPORT BUS PK

MERLIN BUSINESS PARK

Newberry Comm Cen

A30

6

MARWOOD ROAD

MARWOOD

B3184

ROAD

A B C D

A
B
C
D
1
2
3
4
5
6
Foxhayes
Exwick Cemetery
Civil Servi
Sports Gr
Redhills
Upper Old
Wheatley Farm
Nadder Brook
Burnets
Brake
Eastdown
Plantation
Wheatley
Playing
Field
Providene
Court
Farm
EXONIA
PARK
School
Crossmead
Conference
Centre
Cadogan
Court
Poscombe
Bridge
John Stocker
Mid Sch
Health
Centre
Rec
Grnd
Franklyn
House
Cowick Barto
Playing Field
St Thom
Ide House
Balls
Farm
Ide Bridge
Alphin Brook
Oak Ma
Farm
West Town
Farm
Cemy
Ide
Pynes
Cottages
A38
A30
B3212
16

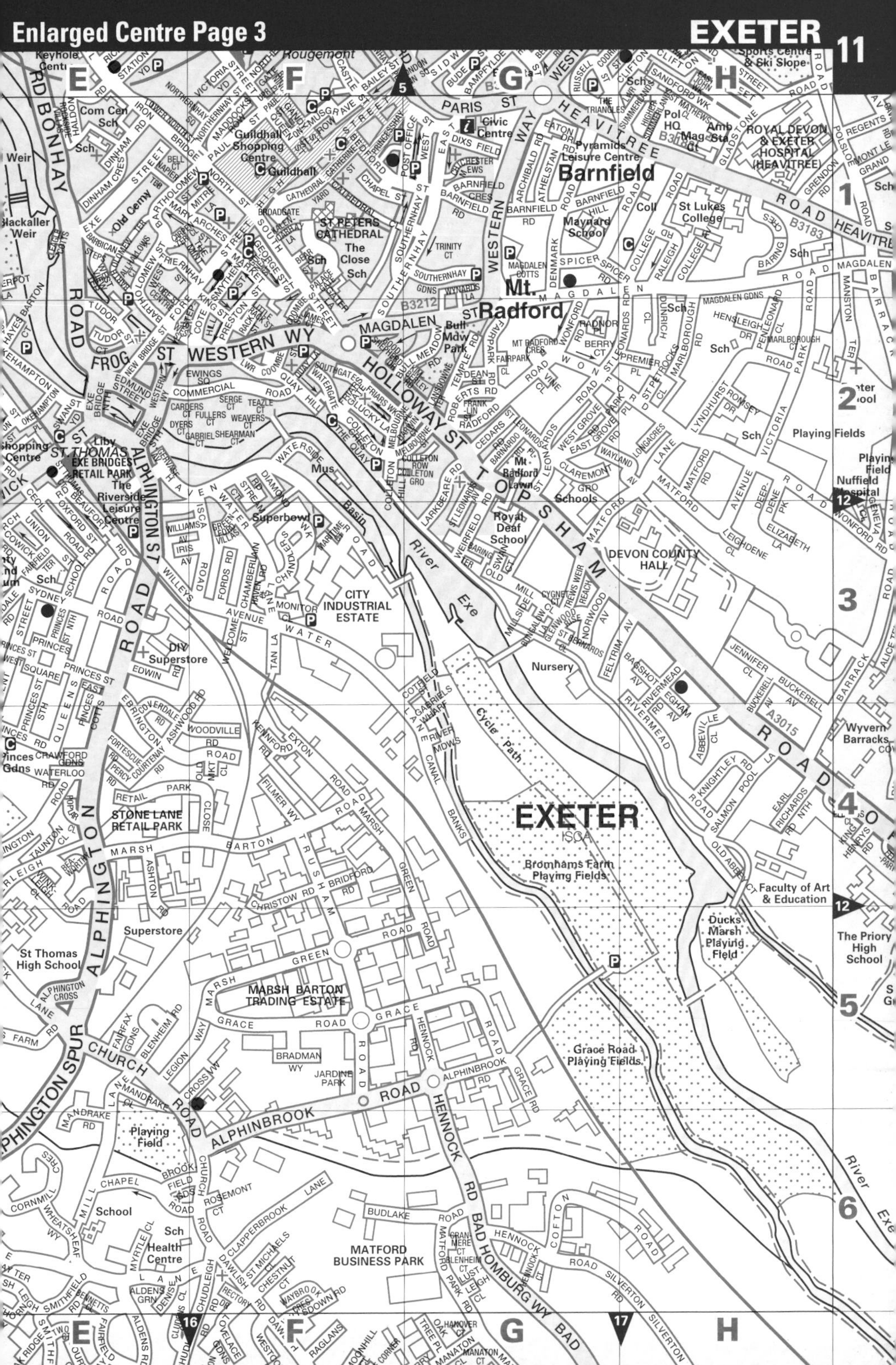
EXETER
ISCA
Barnfield
Mt. Radford
Guildhall Shopping Centre
Guildhall
ST PETERS CATHEDRAL
The Close
Civic Centre
Pyramids Leisure Centre
Maynard School
St Lukes College
ROYAL DEVON & EXETER HOSPITAL (HEAVITREE)
Pol HQ
Mag Ct
Amb Sta
Sports Centre & Ski Slope
Rougemont
Com Cen Sch
Old Cemy
Weir
Blackaller Weir
Shopping Centre
St.THOMAS
EXE BRIDGES RETAIL PARK
The Riverside Leisure Centre
Liby
Superbowl
Mus
Basin
River Exe
CITY INDUSTRIAL ESTATE
DIY Superstore
Royal Deaf School
Mt Radford Lawn
Schools
DEVON COUNTY HALL
Nursery
Cycle Path
Bromhams Farm Playing Fields
Ducks Marsh Playing Field
Faculty of Art & Education
The Priory High School
Wyvern Barracks
Nuffield Hospital
Playing Fields
STONE LANE RETAIL PARK
Superstore
St Thomas High School
MARSH BARTON TRADING ESTATE
Grace Road Playing Fields
Playing Field
School
Health Centre
MATFORD BUSINESS PARK
Bull Mdw Park
ALPHINGTON ROAD
ALPHINGTON ST
ALPHINGTON SPUR
CHURCH ROAD
ALPHINBROOK ROAD
HENNOCK RD
BAD HOMBURG WY
WESTERN WY
HOLLOWAY ST
TOPSHAM ROAD
HEAVITREE ROAD
MAGDALEN RD
WONFORD RD
MATFORD AVENUE
BARRACK RD
PARIS ST
FROG ST
BONHAY RD
COMMERCIAL ROAD
HAVEN RD
WATER LANE
MARSH GREEN ROAD
GRACE ROAD
BARTON ROAD
TRUSHAM ROAD
SILVERTON ROAD
COFTON ROAD
A3015
B3183
B3212
E
F
G
H
1
2
3
4
5
6
5
12
12
16
17

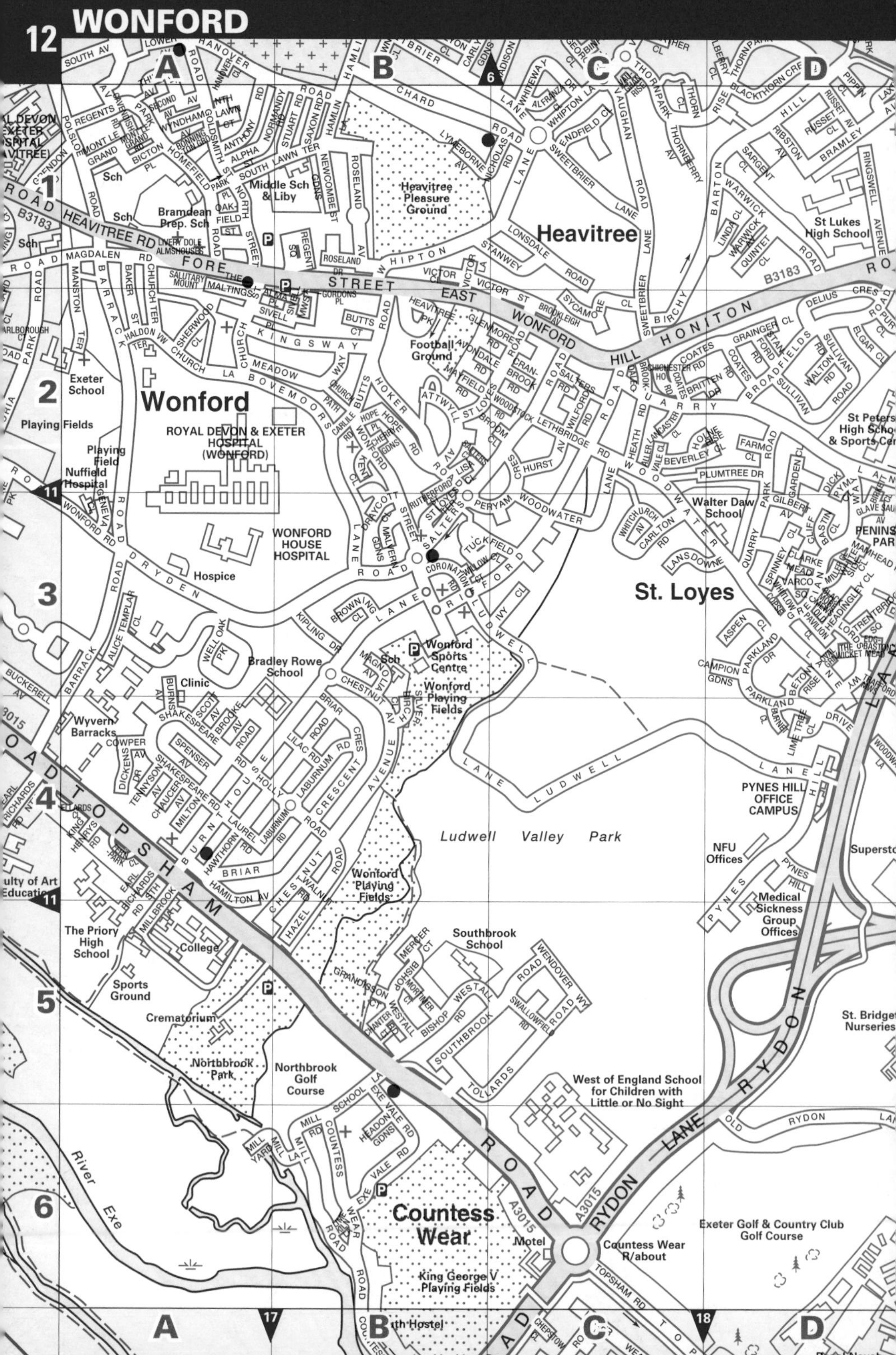
Heavitree
Wonford
St. Loyes
Countess Wear
Heavitree Pleasure Ground
Middle Sch & Liby
Bramdean Prep. Sch
Football Ground
St Lukes High School
Exeter School
Playing Fields
Nuffield Hospital
ROYAL DEVON & EXETER HOSPITAL (WONFORD)
WONFORD HOUSE HOSPITAL
Hospice
Bradley Rowe School
Wonford Sports Centre
Wonford Playing Fields
Wyvern Barracks
Clinic
Walter Daw School
St Peters High School & Sports Centre
PYNES HILL OFFICE CAMPUS
NFU Offices
Medical Sickness Group Offices
Ludwell Valley Park
Southbrook School
The Priory High School
College
Sports Ground
Crematorium
Northbrook Park
Northbrook Golf Course
West of England School for Children with Little or No Sight
Exeter Golf & Country Club Golf Course
Countess Wear R/about
Motel
King George V Playing Fields
St. Bridget Nurseries
River Exe
HEAVITREE RD
FORE STREET
EAST WONFORD HILL
HONITON ROAD
TOPSHAM ROAD
RYDON LANE
B3183
A3015
A
B
C
D
1
2
3
4
5
6
17
18
11
6

E   F   G   H

Radio Hotel
Park & Ride

HONITON ROAD A3015

CHANDSTOCK CL

MEMBURY
DOTTON CL
McCRORY
GITTISHAM
ALDERSON

BARTON RD

gswell
Park

Police Training College

CHELSEA TRADING ESTATE

BITTERN RD
BITTERN IND UNITS

SWAN UNITS

SOWTON INDUSTRIAL ESTATE

CYGNET
CYGNET
HERON

HERON IND UNITS

MALLARD   ROAD

Oak House

Police Sports Ground

Exeter Arms Hotel

QUARRY

LANE

SIDMOUTH   LANE

Buses Only

DIGBY & SOWTON

FALCON   ROAD
Park & Ride
FALCON RD
HARRIER WY

Development

Park & Ride

Rydon Park Caravan Park

BISHOPS CT QUARRY TRADING ESTATE

Bishops Court Sand Quarry

DIGBY
CLYST HEATH
North Grange
South Grange
ELTONHURSTS
BAXTER CL
WRIGHTS CL
LEWIS CRES
COOPER
RUSSELL
WAY
CLYST HALT
APPLE FARM GROVE
AVENUE

MEADOWS

Sandy Park

OLD RYDON LEY
RYDON

OLD RYDON

Depot

Newcourt House

AVOCET RD
OSPREY RD

DCC Depot

PO Sorting Office

DIY Superstore

KINGFISHER WY
OSPREY

The Alpha Centre
S.W.E.B

Depot

ABBEY CT

KESTREL WY

EAGLE

LANE

M5

WAY

PARK FIVE BUSINESS CENTRE

EXETER SERVICES
i

Hotel

MOOR

LANE

A376

Sandy Gate

M5 JUNCTION 30

SIDMOUTH

ROAD

SANDYGATE ROAD

LANE

CLYST

River Clyst

Grindle Brook

Newcourt Barton

Sowton Brake

LANE SOWTON

Sowton 1

Sowton Barton

14

Clyst Valley

2

3

Half Moon Inn

BISHOPS COURT ROAD   BISHO

LANE
TUGELA

THE MANOR PARK

VILLAGE
Sch

CLYST
ST MA

A3052

Clys

Mill Dov 4

WINSLADE PARK AV

14

Football Grnd

Winslade Barton

Winslade Park

CLYS
VALLEY

5

EXMOUTH RD

6

E   F   G   H

Golf Course   18

Cotts Farm

19

Old Winslade

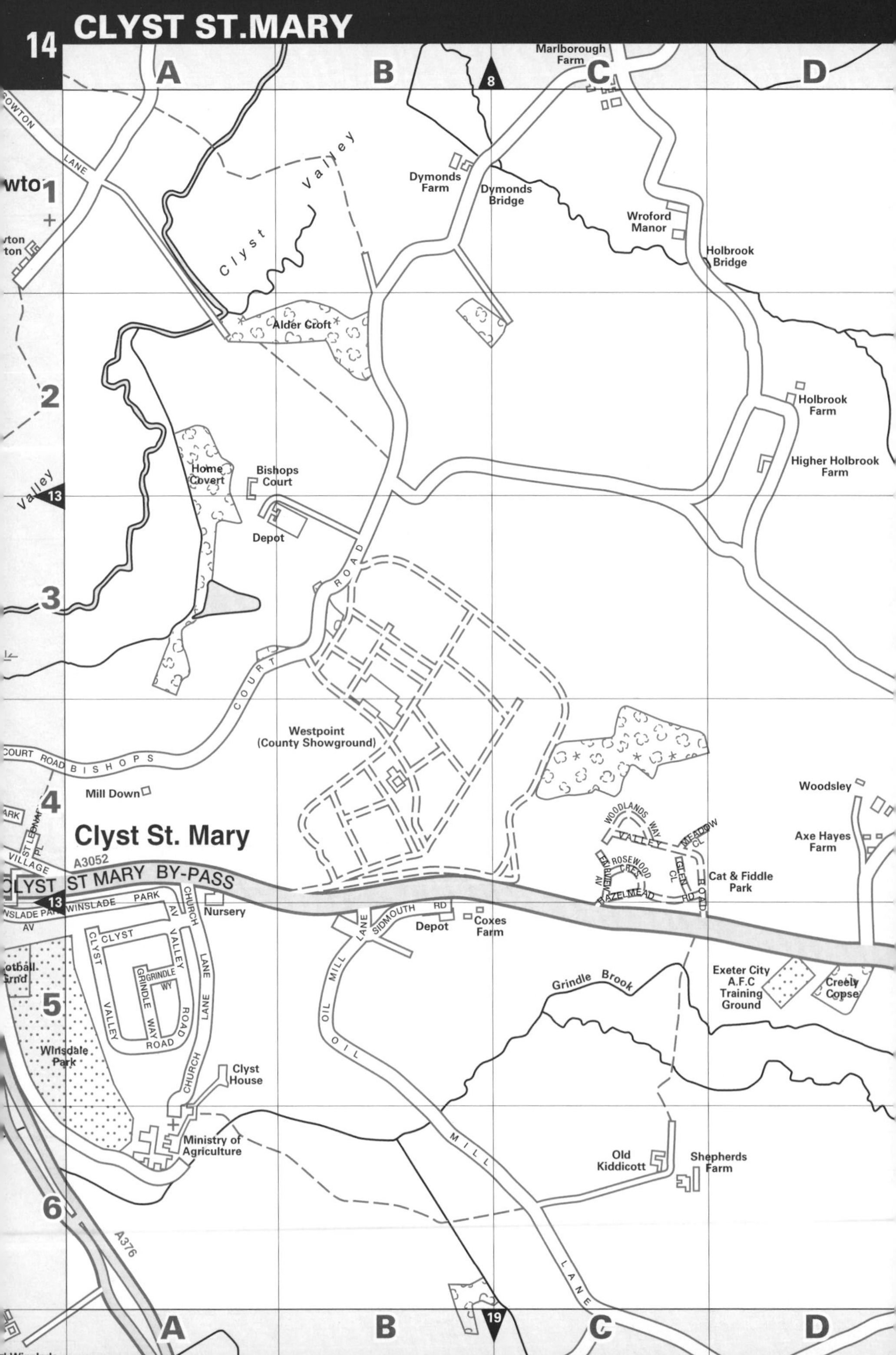

A   B   C   D

Marlborough
Farm

Dymonds
Farm

Dymonds
Bridge

Wroford
Manor

Holbrook
Bridge

Clyst valley

Alder Croft

Holbrook
Farm

Higher Holbrook
Farm

Home
Covert

Bishops
Court

Depot

ROAD

Westpoint
(County Showground)

Woodsley

COURT ROAD BISHOPS

Mill Down

Axe Hayes
Farm

Clyst St. Mary

A3052

WOODLANDS WAY

VALLEY

MEADOW

ROSEWOOD

Cat & Fiddle
Park

HAZELMEAD

CLYST ST MARY BY-PASS

WINSLADE PARK

Nursery

Clyst
House

CLYST VALLEY

GRINDLE WY

CHURCH LANE

SIDMOUTH RD

OIL MILL LANE

Depot

Coxes
Farm

Grindle Brook

Exeter City
A.F.C
Training
Ground

Creely
Copse

Winslade
Park

Clyst
House

Ministry of
Agriculture

OIL

MILL LANE

Old
Kiddicott

Shepherds
Farm

A376

1 2 3 4 5 6

13

8

19

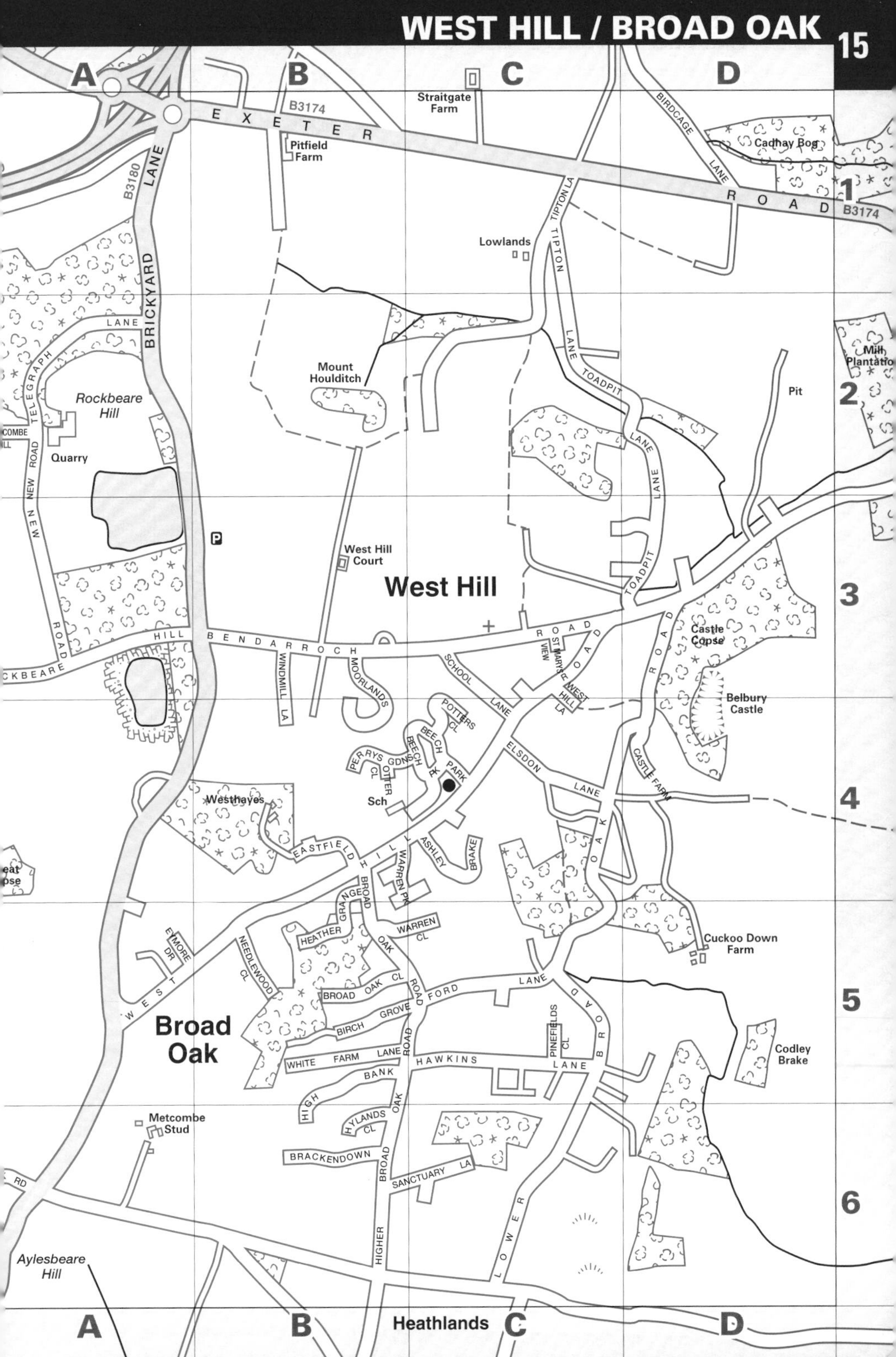
A
B
C
D
1
2
3
4
5
6
B3174
EXETER ROAD
B3180
BRICKYARD LANE
Straitgate Farm
Pitfield Farm
BIRDCAGE LANE
Cadhay Bog
TIPTON LA
TIPTON LANE
Lowlands
TELEGRAPH LANE
Rockbeare Hill
Quarry
NEW ROAD
Mount Houlditch
TOADPIT LANE
Pit
West Hill Court
West Hill
ROCKBEARE HILL
BENDARROCH ROAD
WINDMILL LA
MOORLANDS
SCHOOL LANE
VIEW
ST MARYS
WEST HILL LA
WEST HILL ROAD
Castle Copse
Belbury Castle
POTTERS CL
BEECH PK
BEECH PARK
PERRYS GDNS
OTTER CL
Sch
ELSDON LANE
CASTLE FARM
Westhayes
EASTFIELD
ASHLEY BRAKE
WARREN PK
WARREN CL
GRANGE
BROAD OAK ROAD
HEATHER
Cuckoo Down Farm
EYMORE DR
NEEDLEWOOD CL
BROAD OAK CL
FORD LANE
WEST
Broad Oak
BROAD OAK
BIRCH GROVE
WHITE FARM LANE
PINEFIELDS CL
HAWKINS LANE
Codley Brake
BANK
HIGH
HYLANDS CL
Metcombe Stud
BRACKENDOWN
SANCTUARY LA
HIGHER BROAD OAK
LOWER
RD
Aylesbeare Hill
Heathlands
Mill Plantation

A
B
C
D
10
11
1
2
3
4
5
6
A30
A379
A38
MARKHAM LANE
BARTON
The Barton
Matford Brook
Pengellys
Shillingford Lodge
BARRACK LA
OAK CL
WAYBROOK LANE
Shillingford Abbot
SHILLINGFORD ROAD
CHUDLEIGH ROAD
CHANTRY
MEADOW
DAWLISH
MUTTON
Matford Barton
Peamore Wood
Shillingford Plantation
Peamore House
Little Silve Plantatio
DAYS-POTTLES
MANSTREE
MANSTREE RD
THE WILLOWS
ASH CT
ST GEORGES TER
ILEX CL
Shillingford St. George
Rec Grnd
Place Farm
Shillingford Wood
SHILLINGFORD
Dadmouth
LANE
Kenbury Wood
OLD DAWLISH RD
HAWTHORN WY
OAK RIDGE
SMITHFIELD
TWO ACRE CT
COURTENAY GDNS
FAIRFIELD
ARUNDEL CL
BENNETTS CL
TOTTONS CT
BARNSTONE CT
LACKABOROUGH CT
ALDENS RD
ROYAL VIEW CL
CHUDLEIGH RD
DEACON CL
VELACE GDNS
RECTORY DR
WESTCOMBE
VESTRY DR
CANON WY
HAMMOND CROFT WY
WESLEY WY
STEEPLE DR
LICHGATE RD
PULPIT WK
TOWER WK
RAGLANS
LORAM WAY
MOONHILL CL
THREE CORNER PL
STRAWBERRY AV
KENBURY DR
OTTER CT
WILLSDOWN RD
WAYBROOK CRES

EXMINSTER

- King George V Playing Fields
- Youth Hostel
- Countess Wear Bridge
- Couhtess Wear Bridge
- Countess Wear Combined School
- SILVERTON RD
- SILVERTON ROAD
- MATFORD PARK
- YEOFORD
- WAY
- BAD HOMBURG WAY
- BURG WY BAD HOMBURG
- Exeter Livestock Market
- Matford Park
- Park & Ride
- P
- Matford Marshes
- Towing Path
- B3123 WAY
- DAWLISH ROAD
- ROAD
- owle Hill
- Matford Bridge
- Matford Brook
- Matford Road
- Matford Mews
- Devon Motel
- Matford Home Farm
- Matford House
- DAWLISH LANE
- A379
- BRIDGE ROAD
- DAWLISH ROAD
- Matford Park Farm
- Highfield
- SANNERVILLE WAY
- A379
- Church Path Hill Plantation
- MATFORD LANE
- MAIN RD
- MAIN RD
- SANNE
- M5
- Exminster
- LITTLE SILVER LANE
- LITTLE SILVER LANE
- A30
- MILLER WAY
- EAGER WAY
- REDDAWAY WAY
- RISE
- FARMHOUSE
- ROUGEMONT CT
- Playing Fields
- REDDAWAY DR
- SWAN PRIDEHAM WY
- GROVE CL
- WALNUT CL
- PENNY BROWNLEY CL
- DRIVE
- GLEBELANDS
- Stowey Arms P.H.
- MILBURY RD
- EXMINSTER RD
- CL
- MILBUR
- TAPS CL
- GISSONS L
- 18
- M5 JUNCTION 31
- DEEPWAY LANE
- DAYS POTTLES LA
- YS-POTTLES LA
- FARMHOUSE
- BUCKNOLE CL
- HOLLE CL
- TOWNFIELD
- CREST
- Sch
- DEEPWAY
- MAIN LANE
- MILLETS CL
- OAK CL
- DEEPWAY GDNS
- FOWLER CL
- TOWNEND CL
- DRYFIELD
- Cemy
- CHURCH STILE
- Sunningdale Close
- Playing Field
- SOUTH VIEW TER
- C
- CROCKWELLS ROAD
- DAIRY
- MILESTONES COTTS
- Pottles Wood
- SPURWAY HILL
- TOWSINGTON LANE
- MAIN LANE
- POTTLES CL
- EXMINSTER HILL
- CROCKWELLS RD
- RIVIERA TER
- JUPES CL
- RIVIER
- WESTF
- ANDYWAY
- HER DEVEWAY
- 18

Grid references: E, F, G, H (columns); 1, 2, 3, 4, 5, 6 (rows)

11 · 12 · 18

Lower
Wear

Golf Course

Royal Naval
Stores Depot

Countess Wear
Combined School

The Sheep
Field

Newport
Gardens

Newport Mobile
Homes Park

Sewage
Works

Sludge
Beds

Nature Reserve

Viaduct

M5

Topsham
A.F.C.
Ground

Sainthill
Nurseries

Broom Park
Nurseries

Rugby
Ground

Highfield
Farm

Cem

TOPSHAM

Rec
Grnd

Fire Sta

Exeter Canal

Milbury
Lane

SANNERVILLE WAY

Camy

Museum

Exminster
Marshes
Bird
Sanctuary

RIVER EXE

Cotts
Farm

Station

A379

Lower Duck St

E · 13 · F · G · 14 · H

1

2

3

4

5

6

Old Winslade Farm

Courtbrook Farm

River Clyst

A376

Ford

Clyst St. George

PYTTE GDNS

Clyst St.George Nature Garden

Bushayes corner

LANE

WOODBURY

EXMOUTH RD

CHAPEL HILL

ROAD

Court Farm

MARSH

Knowle House

Fire Brigade H.Q.

Sch

WOODBURY ROAD

B3179 ROAD

Topsham

Weir

Bridge Mill

Clyst Bridge

Dart Farm Shopping Village

DART BUSINESS PARK

Boat Yard

Odhams Wharf

Odams Wharf

Ebford

EBFORD

EBFORD LANE

OLD EBFORD

THE RIDINGS

LOWER LANE

LANE

Ebford Barton

Ebford Manor

GROVE RD

ELM GROVE

ELM GDNS

ELM GROVE

BRIDGE HILL

ELM GROVE RD

MAIN ST

ALTAMIRA

ALTAMIRA STREET

HIGHER SHAPTER ST

LOWER SHAPTER ST

P

BOWLING GREEN ROAD

MOUNT

RIVERSMEET

Western Fields

Bowling Green Marshes Nature Reserve (R.S.P.B)

RIVER CLYST

EXMOUTH LANE

EXMOUTH

EXMOUTH ROAD

HAMPSTEAD LANE

GREEN LANE

GREEN

A376

TRESILLIAN GDNS

ST LLOYD

HILL LA

DADLY LANE

HILL

E · F · G · 20 · H

B

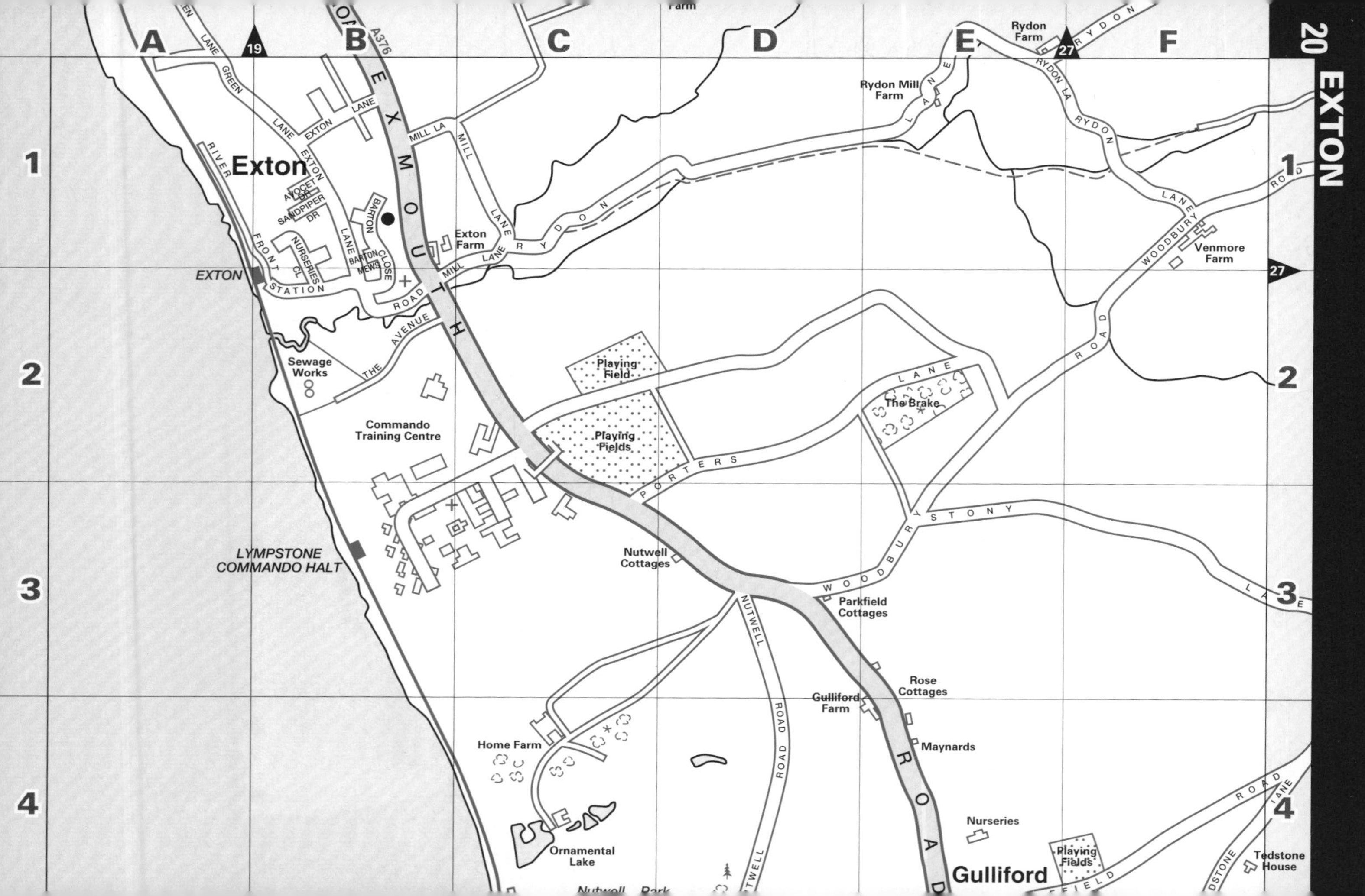

Tedstone House

Playing Fields

Gulliford

Nurseries

Maynards

Rose Cottages

Gulliford Farm

Parkfield Cottages

ROAD

NUTWELL

NUTWELL ROAD

Nutwell Cottages

Home Farm

Ornamental Lake

Nutwell Park

The Brake

Venmore Farm

WOODBURY ROAD

STONY LANE

PORTERS LANE

Playing Field

Playing Fields

Rydon Farm

27

Rydon Mill Farm

RYDON LANE

RYDON LANE

Exton Farm

MILL LANE

EXETON LANE

GREEN LANE

BARTON CLOSE

NURSERIES CL

FRONT

EXTON STATION

River Exton

A376

EXMOUTH

Exton

Commando Training Centre

Sewage Works

THE AVENUE

STATION ROAD

LYMPSTONE COMMANDO HALT

19

5 **6** 24 **7** A-la-Ronde (NT) **8**

SWEET APRIL LANE
ELM CL
ASH GRO
CRESCENT

Watton Brook
Watton Bridge

LANE WOT

LANE

Courtlands Cross

SUMMER LA

RIVERMEAD

ELMFIELD
SYLVAN CL

LITTLEMEAD

A376

LAMP ROAD

THORN CL
R'NFIELD

FEATHERBED LA

FEATHERBED LANE

TEDSTONE

TEDSTONE LANE

WOTTON

Harefield
(St Peters School)

Potters
Farm

ROAD EXETER ROAD EXE

SEAFIELD AVENUE

MARINE

VICTORIA LANE

F

XMOUTH

Thorn Farm

JUBILEE GRO
MALT FIELD ROAD

MEADOW CL

HAREFIELD CL

LANE

Mount
Pleasant

LANE COURTLANDS

LONGBROOK

Courtlands

E

HILL

LANE

Lympstone Grange

GRANGE CL
GLEBELANDS
RABERRY

BIRCH RD

STONE LA

LANE

DAWLISH PK TER

22

Lympstone

D

SIDNEURGH CRES
MEETING
GLEN
GIBRALTAR
TRAFALGAR

HUNTLEY
RD CL

ORCHARD CL

SCHOOL
Sch

ROAD

LONGM

STRAWBERRY

LANE

Sowden
Farm

Mussel
Purifaction
Station

SOWDEN

UNDERHILL
CL
UNDERHILL CT

Daniel's
Corner

NUTWELL

BIRCHMANS
HILL

GREENHILL AV

LYMPSTONE HILL

CHURCH

CHURCH HILL

LAND

UNDERHILL CRES

HIGHCLIFF CL
HIGHCLIFFE CT

C

BURGMANS

CHAPEL LA

SOWDEN LANE

P

Lympstone

Darling's
Rock

QUAY THE

SOWDEN

Lympstone Lake

Lympstone

B

The Ridge

EXE

RIVER

A

5 **6** **7** **8**

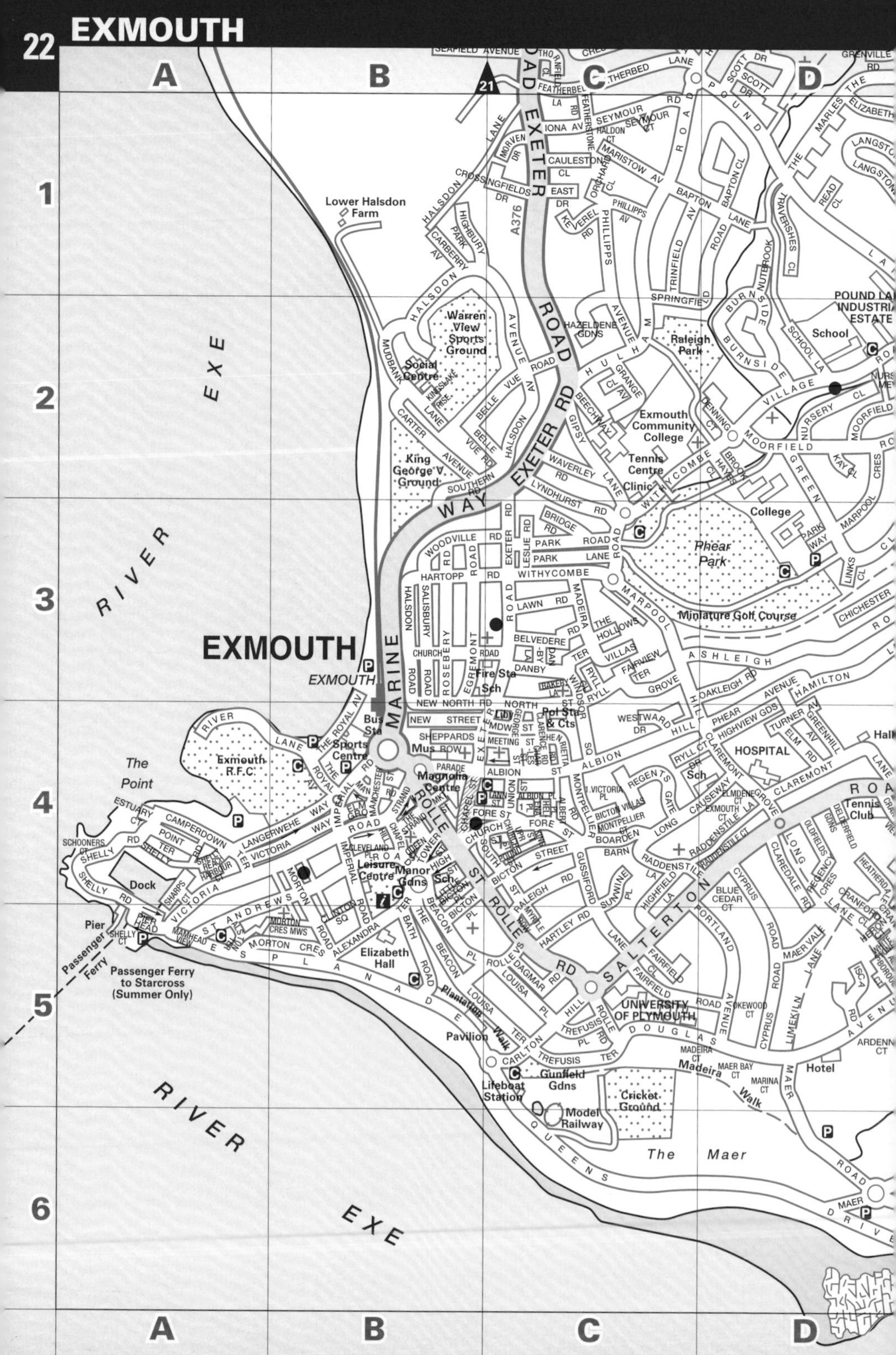
A
B
C
D
1
2
3
4
5
6
21
EXMOUTH
EXMOUTH
RIVER EXE
RIVER EXE
The Point
Lower Halsdon Farm
Warren View Sports Ground
Social Centre
King George V Ground
Exmouth R.F.C.
Sports Centre
Bus Sta
Mus
Magnolia Centre
Fire Sta
Sch
Lby
Pol Sta & Cts
HOSPITAL
Exmouth Community College
Tennis Centre
Clinic
Raleigh Park
Phear Park
College
School
POUND LANE INDUSTRIAL ESTATE
Miniature Golf Course
Dock
Pier
Passenger Ferry
Passenger Ferry to Starcross (Summer Only)
Leisure Centre
Manor Gdns
Elizabeth Hall
Pavilion
Lifeboat Station
Gunfield Gdns
Model Railway
Cricket Ground
UNIVERSITY OF PLYMOUTH
The Maer
Tennis Club
Hotel
EXETER ROAD
EXETER RD
MARINE WAY
ROLLE ST
SALTERTON RD
ESPLANADE
QUEENS DRIVE
Madeira Walk
Plantation Walk
A376

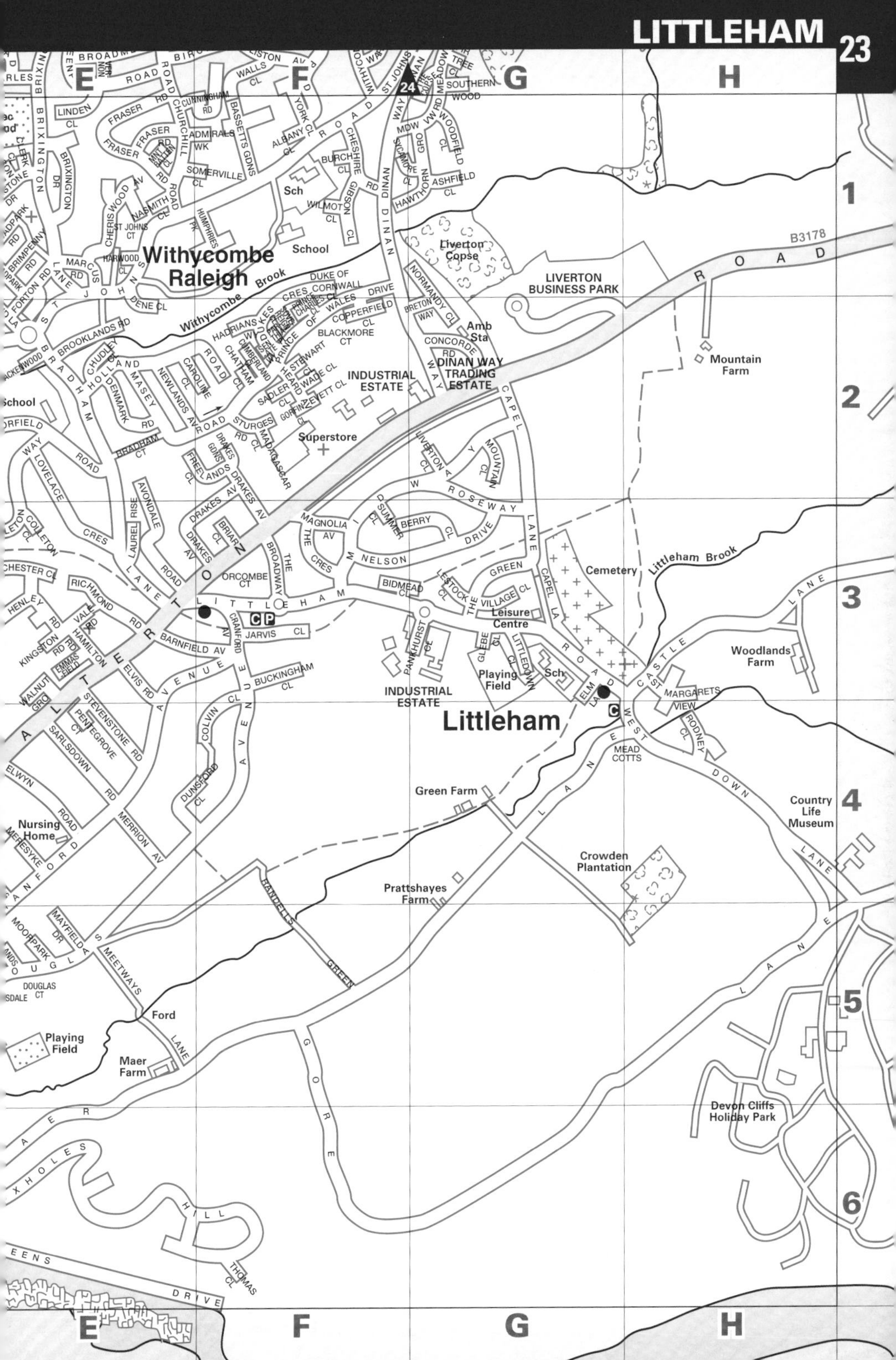
E
F
G
H
1
2
3
4
5
6
Withycombe Raleigh
Littleham
Withycombe Brook
Littleham Brook
B3178
LIVERTON BUSINESS PARK
Liverton Copse
Mountain Farm
DINAN WAY TRADING ESTATE
INDUSTRIAL ESTATE
Superstore
Amb Sta
School
Sch
Cemetery
Leisure Centre
Playing Field
Woodlands Farm
Country Life Museum
Crowden Plantation
Green Farm
Prattshayes Farm
Devon Cliffs Holiday Park
Nursing Home
Ford
Maer Farm
MEAD COTTS
ST MARGARETS VIEW
SALTERTON ROAD
LITTLEHAM ROAD
CASTLE LANE
DOWN LANE
WEST DOWN LANE
CAPEL LANE
GORE LANE
HANDELLS GREEN
MEETWAYS
DOUGLAS AV
DOUGLAS CT
QUEENS DRIVE
MAER LANE
FOXHOLES HILL
THOMAS CL
BRADHAM LANE
ST JOHNS RD
DINAN WAY
MEADOW WAY
SOUTHERN WOOD
ROSEWAY DRIVE
NELSON WAY
DRAKES AV
CRANFORD AV
JARVIS CL
BUCKINGHAM CL
COLVIN CL
DUNSFORD CL
MERRION AV
STEVENSTONE RD
PENTEGROVE CT
SARLSDOWN RD
ELVIS RD
BARNFIELD AV
RICHMOND RD
HAMILTON RD
KINGSTON RD
HENLEY RD
WALNUT GRO
EMMAS FIELD
LAUREL RISE
AVONDALE ROAD
LOVELACE CRES
BRIXINGTON LANE
BROOKLANDS RD
HOLLAND ROAD
DENMARK RD
MASEY RD
NEWLANDS AV
CAROLINE CL
CHATHAM CL
STURGES RD
MADAGASCAR CL
FREELANDS CL
DRAKES GDNS
BRIAR CL
ORCOMBE CT
THE BROADWAY
THE CRES
MAGNOLIA AV
BERRY CL
SUMMER CL
BIDMEAD CL
LESTOCK CL
THE GREEN
THE VILLAGE CL
GLEBE CL
LITTLEDOWN CL
ELM LA
RODNEY CL
PANKHURST CL
LIVERTON CL
MOUNTAIN CL
CONCORDE RD
BRETON WAY
NORMANDY CL
COPPERFIELD CL
BLACKMORE CT
DUKE OF CORNWALL CL
PRINCE OF WALES DRIVE
HADRIANS WY
STEWART CL
HEARD CL
WADE CL
ZEVETT CL
SADLER CL
GORFIN CL
DENE CL
MARCUS RD
HARWOOD CL
ST JOHNS CT
CHERISWOOD AV
NASMITH CL
HUMPHRIES PK
SOMERVILLE CL
ADMIRALS WK
FRASER RD
CHURCHILL RD
BASSETTS GDNS
ALBANY CL
YORK CL
BURCH CL
CHESHIRE RD
GIBSON CL
WILMOT CL
HAWTHORN CL
ASHFIELD CL
WOODFIELD CL
LINDEN CL
BRIXINGTON DR
CUNNINGHAM RD
WALLS CL
RICHMOND RD
MAYFIELD DR
MOORPARK
ELWYN ROAD
MERESYKE
Playing Field
24

House
Monday Copse
Barn Close
Clear View
Coombe Plantation
Lympstone Common
B3179
WRIGHTS LANE
Squabmoor Plantation
Withycombe Raleigh Common
Exe View Wood
EXE VIEW ROAD
Marley Hayes
MARLEY DRIVE
Bystock Wood
Big Wood
Pond
Watton Bridge
WOTTON LANE
Marley Beeches
Goodmores Farm
The Lawn
Bakenhayes
Great Wood
Knucklebones Wood
Dogs Plantation
Ponds
Bystock
Bystock
Withycombe Barton
ST. JOHNS FARM MEWS
SUMMER LANE
The Point in View
A-la-Ronde (NT)
Brixington
Playing Field
Knappe Cross
Hulham
Schools
Higher Veiges Plantation
Lower Veiges Plantation
A376

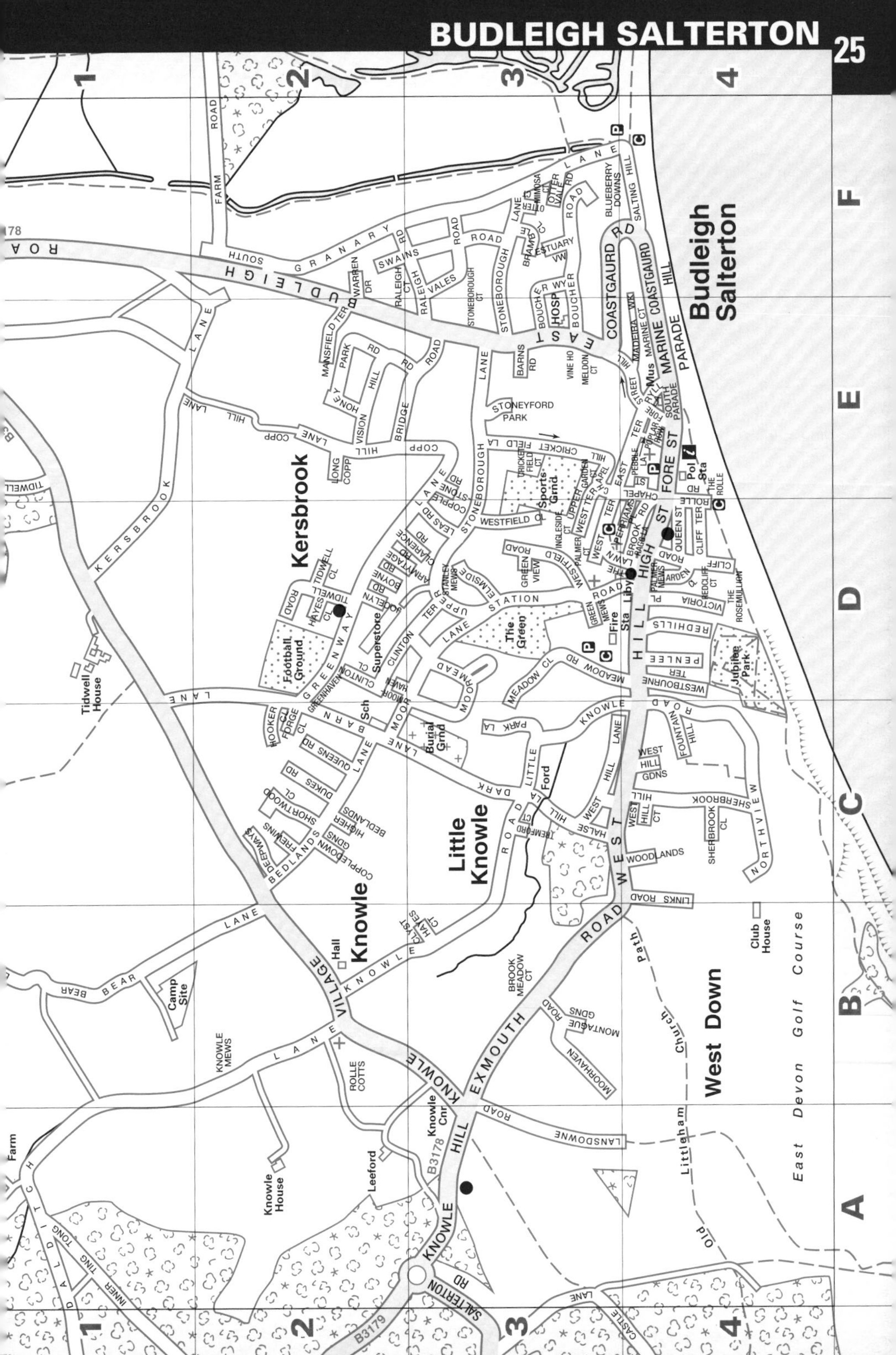
Budleigh Salterton
Kersbrook
Little Knowle
Knowle
West Down
East Devon Golf Course
Tidwell House
Knowle House
Leeford
Knowle Cnr
Camp Site
Hall
Football Ground
Superstore
Sch
Burial Grnd
The Green
Sports Grnd
Jubilee Park
Club House
Fire Sta
Liby
Pol Sta
Mus
Hosp
Ford
Stoneyford Park
Budleigh Road
East Budleigh Road
Exmouth Road
Knowle Hill
Knowle Village
High St
Fore St
Marine Parade
Coastguard Rd
Station Road
West Hill
Dark Lane
Copp Hill Lane
Kersbrook Lane
Bear Lane
Greenway
Stoneborough Lane
Granary Lane
Links Road
Lansdowne Road
Salterton Rd
Old Littleham Church Path
B3178
B3179
A B C D E F
1 2 3 4

A B C A379 D

THE P

1 Warbore Plantation
Rifle Range
Staplake Mount
Staplake Rise
STAPLAKE RD

STARCROSS

BRICKYARD
COURTENAY ST
LONGFIELD ESTATE
BONHAY CL
WESTWOOD
BONHAY RD

Starcross

BARLEY WK
PEACOCK PL
SERCOMBE
STRAND
Jetty
Passenger

2 Vennbridge Farm
ROAD
DREW
NEW LANE
COOKSONS RD
BRUNEL
SWAN RD
PARKERS ROAD
Sch
CHURCH
Surgery
P
ST ROAD
COURTENAY
ELM
HAMILTON
WESTERN
BISHOPS
COURTESIES LANE
CRESTIES LANE
Rec Grnd
Passenger Ferry to Exmouth (Summer Only)

STAPLAKE LANE
GENERALS
NEW ROAD
GENERALS CL

3 Easter Hill
Oak Meadow Golf Club
ROAD
THE STRAND

ROAD

4 Cofford Farm
LANE CHURCH
VICARAGE RD
COFTON HILL
DAWLISH
COFTON HILL
Sch
SCHOOLS
HILL CRES
COFTON HILL
WESTWOOD HILL
MIDDLEWOOD HILL
WESTWOOD HILL

Cockwood

5 Caravan Park
COFTON
Caravan Park
COFTON
WARREN

EXETER ROAD

6 PORT ROAD
EXETER RD
A379
ORCHARD
LANE
ROAD
Eastdon House

A B C D

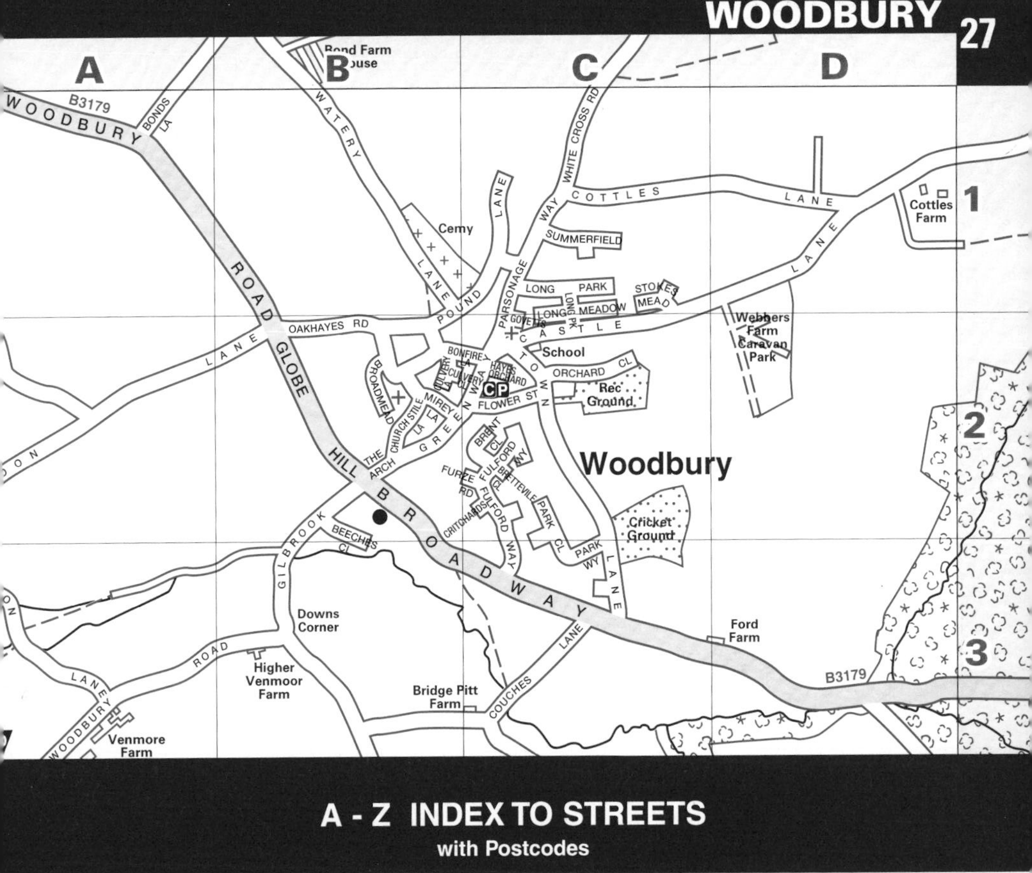

A - Z INDEX TO STREETS
with Postcodes

e Index includes some mes for which there is sufficient space on the aps. These names are dicated by an * and are lowed by the nearest joining thoroughfare.

Black Hat La EX6 10 A3
Blackall Rd EX4 3 C2
Blackboy Rd EX4 5 H6
Blackhorse La EX1 7 G5
Blackmore Ct EX8 23 F2
Blackmore Mews EX2 12 D3
Blackthorn Cres EX1 12 D1
Blenheim Ct EX2 11 G6
Blenheim Rd EX2 11 E5
Blue Cedar Ct EX8 22 D4
Blueberry Downs EX9 25 F3
Bluecoat La EX1 3 D4
Boarden Barn EX8 22 C4
Bodley Cl EX1 6 C6
Bonds La EX5 27 A1
Bonfire La EX5 27 B2
Bonhay Cl EX6 26 C1
Bonhay Rd, Exeter EX4 3 A2
Bonhay Rd, Starcross EX6 26 D2
Bonnington Gro EX1 12 A1
Bonville Cl EX1 6 C6
Booth Way EX8 24 A4
Boucher Rd EX9 25 E3
Boucher Way EX9 25 E3
Bourn Rise EX4 7 E3
Bovemoors La EX2 12 A2
Bowe Ct EX1 5 H6
Bowhay La EX4 10 C2
Bowling Green Rd EX3 19 E4
Bowring Cl EX1 6 C6
Boyne Rd EX9 25 D2
Brackendale EX8 24 B3
Brackendown EX11 15 B6
Brackenwood EX8 23 E2
Bradfield Rd EX4 7 E3
Bradford Cl EX8 24 B3
Bradham Ct EX8 23 E2
Bradham La EX8 23 E2
Bradman Way EX2 11 F5
Bradninch Pl EX4 3 C3
Bramble Cl EX9 25 F3
Bramley Av EX1 12 D1
Branscombe Cl EX4 10 B2
Brent Cl EX5 27 C2
Brentor Cl EX4 4 C5
Breton Way EX8 23 F2
Brettevile Cl EX5 27 C2
Briar Cl EX8 23 F3
Briar Cres EX2 12 A4
Brickyard La, Exeter EX6 26 C2
Brickyard La, Ottery St Mary EX11 15 A2
Bridespring Rd EX4 6 A4
Bridespring Walk EX4 6 A4
Bridford Rd EX2 11 F4
Bridge Cotts EX4 5 G5
Bridge Ct EX4 3 B4
Bridge Hill EX3 19 E4
Bridge Rd, Budleigh Salterton EX9 25 E2
Bridge Rd, Exeter EX2 17 G2
Bridge Rd, Exmouth EX8 22 C3
Bridgehill Garth EX3 19 E4
Brimpenny Rd EX8 23 E1
Brittany Ho EX4 3 D3
Brittany Rd EX8 24 B3
Britten Dr EX2 12 C2
Brixington Dr EX8 23 E1
Brixington La EX8 24 B4
Broad Oak Rd EX11 15 B4
Broad Vw EX5 9 B2
Broadfield Rd EX2 12 D2
Broadgate EX1 3 C4
Broadleaf Cl EX1 7 F4
Broadmead, Exeter EX5 27 B2
Broadmead, Exmouth EX8 24 C4
Broadmeadow Av EX4 10 D3
Broadoak Cl EX11 15 B5
Broadpark Rd EX8 23 E1
Broadparks Av EX4 7 F3
Broadparks Cl EX4 7 F3
Broadwalk Ho EX1 3 D4
Broadway, Exeter EX2 10 C4
Broadway, Woodbury EX5 27 B2
Brodick Cl EX4 5 H4
Brook Cl EX1 6 D5
Brook Green Ter EX4 5 G5
Brook Meadow Ct EX9 25 B3
Brook Rd EX9 25 D4
Brookdale EX2 12 C2
Brooke Av EX2 12 A4
Brookfield Gdns EX2 11 E6
Brookhayes Cl EX8 22 D2
Brooklands Rd EX8 23 E2
Brookleigh Av EX1 12 C2
Brookside Cres EX4 6 C3
Brookway EX1 6 D5
Broom Cl EX2 12 B2
Browning Cl EX2 12 B3
Brownlees EX6 17 G5
Brunel Cl EX4 3 A2
Brunel Rd EX6 26 C2
Brunswick St EX4 3 A6
Buckerell Av EX2 11 H3
Buckingham Cl EX8 23 F3
Buckleigh Cl EX4 7 E3
Bucknill Cl EX6 17 H5
Buddle La EX4 10 D2
Bude St EX1 3 D3
Budlake Rd EX2 11 F6
Bull Meadow Rd EX2 3 D5
Buller Rd EX4 3 A6
Bungalow La EX2 11 G3
Bunn Rd EX8 24 C3
Burch Cl EX8 23 F1
Burgmanns Hill EX8 21 C5
Burnet Cl EX2 12 D4
Burns Av EX2 12 A3
Burnside EX8 22 D2
Burnthouse La EX2 12 A4
Burrator Dr EX4 4 C5
Burrow Rd EX5 9 B1
Butts Ct EX2 12 B2
Butts Rd EX2 12 B2
Byron Rd EX2 13 E2
Byron Way EX8 24 B3
Bystock Cl EX4 3 B3
Bystock Mews EX8 24 D3
Bystock Rd EX8 24 C3
Bystock Ter EX4 3 B3

California Cl EX4 5 G2
Calthorpe Rd EX4 6 B4
Cambridge St EX4 3 A5
Camelot Cl EX4 6 B4
Camperdown Ter EX8 22 A4
Campion Gdns EX2 12 C3
Canal Banks EX2 11 G4
Canberra Cl EX4 5 H2
Canon Way EX2 16 C1
Canterbury Rd EX4 4 C6
Canterbury Way EX8 24 D3
Capel La EX8 23 G2
Carberry Av EX8 22 B1
Carders Ct EX2 3 B6
Carfax EX1 3 C4
Carlile Rd EX2 12 B2
Carlton Hill EX8 22 C5
Carlton Rd EX2 12 C3
Carlyon Cl EX1 6 B6
Carlyon Gdns EX1 6 B6
Caroline Cl EX8 23 E2
Carpenter Cl EX4 3 B4
Carter Av EX8 22 B2
Castle Farm EX11 15 D4
Castle La, Exeter EX5 27 C2
Castle La, Exmouth EX8 23 H3
Castle Mount EX4 3 C2
Castle St EX4 3 C3
Cathedral Cl EX1 3 C4
Cathedral Yd EX1 3 C4
Catherine St EX1 3 C4
Cauleston Cl EX8 22 C1
Causey Gdns EX1 7 F3
Causey La EX1 7 F4
Cavendish Rd EX1 12 A1
Cecil Rd EX2 3 A6
Cedar Cl EX8 24 C3
Cedars Rd EX2 3 D6
Celia Cres EX4 6 B2
Cemetery Pl EX4 3 B4
Central Av, Exeter EX4 6 C3
Central Av, Lower Wear EX2 18 B2
Chamberlain Rd EX2 11 F3
Chancel Ct EX4 7 E3
Chancel La EX4 7 E3
Chancellors Way EX4 6 B2
Chandlers Walk EX2 11 F3
Chanter Ct EX2 12 B5
Chantry Mdw EX2 16 C1
Chapel Hill, Budleigh Salterton EX9 25 E3
Chapel Hill, Exeter EX3 19 G3
Chapel Hill, Exmouth EX8 22 B4
Chapel Rd EX2 11 E6
Chapel St, Budleigh Salterton EX9 25 E4
Chapel St, Exeter EX1 3 D4
Chapel St, Exmouth EX8 22 B4
Chaplel La EX8 21 C6
Chapple Cl EX6 26 D2
Chard Rd EX1 12 B1
Chardstock Cl EX1 13 E1
Charingthay Gate EX4 5 H4
Charles St EX8 22 C4
Charnley Av EX4 10 C2
Chatham Cl EX8 23 F2
Chaucer Av EX2 12 A4
Chaucer Rise EX8 24 A3
Cheeke St EX1 5 G6
Chelmsford Rd EX4 4 B6
Cheltenham Cl EX4 4 B6
Chepstow Cl EX2 17 H1
Cheriswood Av EX8 23 E1
Cherry Cl EX8 24 B3
Cherry Gdns EX2 12 B2
Cherry Tree Cl EX4 5 E2
Cheshire Rd EX8 23 F1
Chester Cl EX4 4 C6
Chestnut Av EX2 12 B3
Chestnut Cl EX8 24 B4
Chestnut Ct EX2 11 F6
Cheyne Rise EX4 7 E3
Cheynegate La EX4 6 D1
Chichester Cl EX8 22 D3
Chichester Ho EX2 12 C2
Chichester Mews EX1 3 D4
Christow Rd EX2 11 F4
Chudleigh Rd EX2 11 F6
Chudley Cl EX8 23 E2
Church Cl EX5 9 B1
Church Hill EX4 6 D1
Church La, Broadclyst EX5 9 B1
Church La, Clyst St Mary EX5 14 A4
Church La, Exeter EX4 3 D3
Church La, Pinhoe EX4 7 E2
Church La, Wonford EX2 12 A2
Church Path EX2 12 B2
Church Path Rd EX2 10 D3
Church Rd, Cockwood EX6 26 B4
Church Rd, Exeter EX2 3 A6
Church Rd, Exmouth EX8 22 B3
Church Rd, Lymstone EX8 21 D6
Church Rd, St Thomas EX2 11 E5
Church Side EX5 8 C5
Church St, Exeter EX2 12 A2
Church St, Exmouth EX8 22 B4
Church St, Starcross EX6 26 C2
Church Stile EX6 17 H5
Church Stile La EX5 27 B2
Church Ter EX2 12 A1
Churchill Ct EX8 21 D5
Churchill Rd, Exeter EX2 10 D3
Churchill Rd, Exmouth EX8 24 C4
Chute St EX1 5 H6
City Arc EX4 3 C5
Clapperbrook La EX2 11 F6
Clara Pl EX3 18 D4
Claredale Rd EX8 22 D4
Claremont Gro, Exeter EX2 11 G2
Claremont Gro, Exmouth EX8 22 D4
Claremont La EX8 22 D4
Clarence Pl EX4 5 G5
Clarence Rd, Budleigh Salterton EX9 25 D3
Clarence Rd, Exeter EX4 3 A6
Clarence Rd, Exmouth EX8 22 C4
Clarke Mead EX2 12 D3
Clay La EX8 21 D6
Clayton Rd EX4 3 A2
Clerk Cl EX8 23 E1
Cleve Rd EX4 4 C6
Clevedon Cl EX4 5 G4
Cleveland Ct EX1 5 H6
Cleveland Pl EX8 22 B4
Cleveland St EX4 3 A6
Cliff Bastin Cl EX2 12 D3
Cliff Rd EX9 25 D4
Cliff Ter EX9 25 D4
Clifford Cl EX1 6 C6
Clifford Rd EX4 6 A5
Clifton Cotts EX1 5 H6
Clifton Hill EX1 5 H6
Clifton Rd EX1 5 H6
Clifton St EX1 5 H6
Clinton Av EX4 6 A5
Clinton Cl EX9 25 D2
Clinton Sq EX8 22 B5
Clinton St EX4 3 A6
Clinton Ter EX9 25 D2
Clipper Quay EX2 3 D6
Cliston Av EX8 24 D4
Cloister Rd EX4 6 A5
Cludens Cl EX2 16 C1
Clydesdale Rd EX4 5 E3
Clyst Halt Av EX2 13 E3
Clyst Hayes Ct EX9 25 B3
Clyst Heath EX2 13 E4
Clyst Rd EX3 13 F5
Clyst St Mary By-Pass EX5 13 H4
Clyst Valley Rd EX5 14 A5
Coastgaurd Hill EX9 25 E4
Coastgaurd Rd EX9 25 E3
Coates Rd EX2 12 C2
Codrington St EX1 5 G6
Cofton Hill EX6 26 C5
Cofton La EX6 26 B5
Cofton Rd EX2 11 G6
Colands Ct EX2 16 B1
Coleridge Cl EX8 24 B3
Coleridge Rd EX2 10 D3
College Av EX1 11 H1
College La EX2 10 A5
College Rd EX1 11 H1
Colleton Cl EX8 23 E3
Colleton Cres EX2 3 C6
Colleton Gro EX2 3 D6
Colleton Hill EX2 3 D6
Colleton Mews EX2 3 D6
Colleton Row EX2 3 D6
Colleton Way EX8 23 E3
Collins Rd EX4 5 G3
Colvin Cl EX8 23 F4
Combourg Cl EX8 24 E4
Comercial Rd EX2 3 B5
Comilla Cl EX8 24 B3
Commercial Rd EX4 11 E2
Commins Rd EX1 6 A5
Concorde Rd EX8 23 G2
Coney Ct EX2 3 C6
Coneybeare EX1 6 C6
Conrad Av EX4 6 D4
Cookson Rd EX6 26 C2
Coombe St EX1 11 F2
Copp Hill La EX9 25 E3
Copperfield Cl EX8 23 F2
Coppledown Gdns EX9 25 C2
Copplestone Dr EX4 5 E3
Copplestone Rd EX9 25 D3
Cordery Rd EX2 10 D4
Cornflower Hill EX4 4 B5
Cornmill Cres EX2 11 E6
Cornwall St EX4 3 A5
Coronation Rd EX2 12 B3
Cotfield St EX2 11 G3
Cotterell Rd EX5 8 C2
Cottey Cres EX4 6 B2
Cottles La EX5 27 C1
Couches La EX5 27 C3
Countess Wear Rd EX2 12 B6
Counties Cres EX6 26 D2
Couper Mdws EX2 13 E4
Courtenay Cl EX6 26 C1
Courtenay Gdns EX2 16 C1
Courtenay Rd EX2 11 E4
Courtenay Ter EX6 26 D2
Courtlands La EX8 21 E7
Coventry Rd EX4 4 C6
Coverdale Rd EX2 11 E4
Cowick Hill EX2 10 C4
Cowick La EX2 10 D3
Cowick Rd EX2 11 E3
Cowick St EX4 3 A6
Cowley Bridge Rd EX4 3 A1
Cowley Mede EX4 4 D2
Cowley Vw EX4 5 E3
Cowper Av EX2 12 A4
Coysh Sq EX3 18 D4
Crabb La EX2 10 D5
Cranbrook Rd EX2 12 C2
Cranford Av EX8 22 D5
Cranford Cl EX8 22 D4
Cranford Vw EX8 22 D4
Cranmere Ct EX2 11 G6
Crawford Gdns EX2 11 E4
Creadly La EX3 18 D3
Crediton Rd EX4 4 C1
Creely Cl EX2 16 D1
Cricket Field Ct EX9 25 E3
Cricket Field La EX9 25 E3
Cricklepit St EX1 3 C5
Critchards EX5 27 B2
Crockwells Cl EX6 18 A6
Crockwells Rd EX6 18 A5
Croft Chase EX4 10 B3
Cross View Ter EX2 10 C5
Cross Vw EX2 11 F5
Crossingfields Dr EX8 22 B1
Crowders Hill EX8 24 A3
Culverland Cl EX4 5 H5
Culverland Rd EX4 5 G5
Culvery Cl EX5 27 B2
Culvery La EX5 27 B2
Cumberland Cl EX8 23 F2
Cunningham Rd EX8 23 E1
Curlew Way EX4 5 G3
Cygnet EX2 13 F2
Cygnet Ct EX2 11 G3
Cypress Dr EX4 4 C6
Cyprus Rd EX8 22 D4

Dagmar Rd EX8 22 C5
Dai Cl EX4 3 A1
Dairy Cl EX6 17 H6
Daisy Links EX4 4 B5
Dalditch La EX9 25 A1
Daleside Rd EX4 5 H4
Danby La EX8 22 C3
Danby Ter EX8 22 C3
Dandy La EX4 7 E2
Danes Rd EX4 3 C1
Danesway EX4 7 F3
Dark La EX9 25
Darwin Ct EX2 3
Dawlish Park Ter EX8 21
Dawlish Rd EX2 11
Dawlish Warren Rd EX6 26
Dawn Cl EX1 6
Days-Pottles La EX6 16
De La Rue Way EX4 7
Deacon Cl EX2 16
Dean St EX2 3
Deanery Pl EX1 3
Deepdene Pk EX2 11
Deepway Ct EX6 17
Deepway Gdns EX6 17
Deepway La EX6 17
Deepways EX9 25
Delderfield Gdns EX8 22
Delius Cres EX2 12
Dene Cl EX8 23
Denise Cl EX2 11
Denmark Rd, Exeter EX1 11
Denmark Rd, Exmouth EX8 23
Denning Ct EX8 22
Denver Cl EX3 18
Denver Rd EX3 18
Devon Rd EX4 6
Devonshire Pl EX4 5
Diamond Rd EX2 3
Diane Cl EX8 24
Dick Pym Cl EX2 12
Dickens Dr EX2 12
Digby Dr EX2 13
Dinan Way EX8 24
Dinham Cres EX4 3
Dinham Mews EX4 3
Dinham Rd EX4 3
Dixs Fld EX1 3
Doctors Walk EX2 10
Dorchester Way EX8 24
Doriam Cl EX4 5
Dorset Av EX4 10
Dotton Cl EX1 13
Douglas Av EX8 22
Douglas Ct EX8 23
Dove Way EX2 10
Drake Av EX2 13
Drakes Av EX8 23
Drakes Farm EX2 10
Drakes Gdns EX8 23
Drakes Rd EX4 3
Draycott Cl EX2 12
Drews Cl EX6 26
Dryden Rd EX2 12
Dryfield EX6 17
Ducks Orch EX6 18
Duckworth Rd EX2 10
Duke of Cornwall Cl EX8 23
Dukes Cres EX8 23
Dukes Rd EX9 25
Dunchideock Rd EX2 10
Dunrich Cl EX2 11
Dunsford Cl EX8 23
Dunsford Gdns EX4 10
Dunsford Rd EX2 10
Dunvegan Cl EX4 4
Durham Cl, Exeter EX1 6
Durham Cl, Exmouth EX8 24
Dutch Ct EX3 18
Dyers Ct EX2 3

Eager Way EX6 17
Eagle Cotts EX4 3
Eagle Way EX2 13
Eagles Nest EX2 10
Earl Richards Rd North EX2 11
Earl Richards Rd South EX2 12
East Av EX1 6
East Budleigh Rd EX9 25
East Dr EX8 22
East Grove Rd EX2 11
East John Walk EX1 5
East Ter EX9 25
East View Ter EX4 5
East Wonford Hill EX2 12
Eastern Av EX2 18
Eastfield EX11 15
Eastgate EX1 3
Eaton Dr EX1 11
Ebford La EX3 19
Ebrington Rd EX2 11
Edgbaston Mead EX2 12
Edgerton Park Rd EX4 3
Edinburgh Cres EX8 21
Edinburgh Dr EX4 4
Edmonton Cl EX4 6
Edmund St EX2 3
Edwin Rd EX2 11
Egham Av EX2 11
Egremont Rd EX8 22
Elaine Cl EX4 6
Eldertree Gdns EX4 3
Elgar Cl EX2 12

abeth Av EX4 5 H4
abeth La EX2 11 H3
abeth Rd EX8 22 D1
rds Cl EX2 12 A4
t Way EX2 13 E2
tt Cl EX4 5 H3
ood Rd EX8 24 C4
Cl EX5 9 B2
Ct EX6 26 D2
Gro EX8 22 B4
Gro Rd EX3 18 D3
Grove Av EX3 19 E4
Grove Gdns EX3 19 E4
Grove Rd, xeter EX4 3 B2
Grove Rd, psham EX3 18 D3
La EX8 23 G3
Rd EX8 22 D4
bridge Gdns EX4 5 E4
dene Ct EX8 22 D4
don Cl EX4 5 G4
field Cres EX8 21 F8
side, dleigh Salterton X9 25 D3
side, Exeter EX4 5 H5
side Cl EX4 5 H5
don La EX11 15 C4
n Rd EX4 6 A5
s Rd EX8 23 E3
yn Rd EX8 23 E4
Cl EX4 4 B6
manuel Cl EX4 3 A5
manuel Rd EX4 3 A5
masfield EX8 23 E3
peror Way EX1 7 F6
field Cl EX1 12 C1
dsleigh Cres EX5 8 A5
nerdale Way EX4 4 D6
lanade EX8 22 A5
ex Cl EX4 10 C3
sington Cl EX8 24 A4
uary Ct EX8 22 A4
uary Vw EX9 25 F3
nhurst Cl EX2 13 E4
ergreen Cl EX8 24 C3
ett Cl EX8 23 F2
an Dr EX8 24 D3
ings Sq EX2 3 C5
bridge Ho EX2 3 B5
calibur Cl EX4 6 C4
e Bri North EX2 3 B6
e Bri South EX2 3 B6
e St, Exeter EX4 3 B4
e St, Topsham EX3 18 D4
e Vale Rd EX2 12 B5
e Valley Way EX4 4 D6
e View EX6 17 H5
e View Cotts EX4 4 D5
e View Rd EX8 24 B1
eminster Hill EX6 17 H6
eter Rd, Exeter EX6 26 A6
eter Rd, xmouth EX8 21 F7
eter Rd, ttery St Mary EX11 15 B1
eter Rd, opsham EX3 18 C2
nibition Way EX4 7 E4
mouth Ct EX8 22 D4
mouth Rd, udleigh Salterton X9 25 B3
mouth Rd, xeter EX5 13 H5
mouth Rd, xmouth EX8 21 E5
mouth Rd, xton EX3 20 B1
onia Pk EX2 10 B3
ton La EX3 20 B1
ton Rd EX2 11 F4
wick Ct EX4 4 D5
wick Hill EX4 4 C5
wick La EX4 4 A6
wick Rd EX4 4 D6
wick Villas EX4 4 D6
more Dr EX11 15 A5

ir Oak Cl EX6 9 B3
rfax Gdns EX2 11 E5
rfield Av EX4 6 D5
rfield Cl EX8 22 C5
rfield Rd, xeter EX2 16 C1
rfield Rd, xmouth EX8 22 C5
rfield Ter EX2 11 E3
rhazel Dr EX4 4 C6
rmead Ct EX1 7 F4
rpark Cl EX2 11 G2
rpark Rd EX2 3 D5
irview Av EX5 14 C4
irview Ter, xeter EX1 7 G4
irview Ter, xmouth EX8 22 C3
lcon Rd EX2 13 F3

Falkland Cl EX4 5 H2
Farleys Ct EX3 18 D4
Farm Cl EX2 12 D2
Farm Hill EX4 4 B5
Farmhouse Av EX1 7 F4
Farmhouse Rise EX6 17 G5
Featherbed La EX8 21 F8
Featherstone Rd EX8 22 C1
Feltrim Av EX2 11 G3
Ferndale Gdns EX2 11 E3
Ferndale Rd EX2 11 E3
Fernpark Cl EX2 12 A4
Ferry Rd EX3 18 C4
Filmer Way EX2 11 F4
Fingle Cl EX4 4 C5
Fir Tree Cl EX8 24 E4
Firs Pk EX2 10 A4
First Av, Exeter EX1 6 A6
First Av, Lower Wear EX2 18 B2
Flayes Almshouses EX4 6 D5
Florida Dr EX4 5 G2
Flower St EX5 27 C2
Flowerpot La EX4 3 A5
Follett Rd EX3 18 D4
Ford La EX11 15 C5
Fordland Bottom Rd EX2 10 A6
Fords Rd EX2 11 F3
Fore St, Budleigh Salterton EX9 25 E4
Fore St, Exeter EX4 3 B5
Fore St, Exmouth EX8 22 B4
Fore St, Ide EX2 10 B5
Fore St, Topsham EX3 18 D4
Fore St, Wonford EX1 12 A1
Fore Street Centre EX4 3 B5
Fore Street Hill EX9 25 E4
Forge Cl EX9 25 C2
Fortescue Rd EX2 11 E4
Forton Rd EX8 23 E2
Foundry Ct EX2 3 C6
Fountain Hill EX9 25 C4
Fouracre Cl EX4 6 B4
Fowey Cl EX1 6 A5
Fowler Cl EX6 17 G5
Fox Rd EX4 6 C3
Foxglove Rise EX4 4 B5
Foxhayes Rd EX4 4 D6
Foxholes Hill EX8 23 E6
Foxtor Rd EX4 4 B5
Francis Cl EX4 10 D3
Franklin St EX2 3 D6
Franklyn Cl EX2 10 D4
Franklyn Dr EX2 10 D3
Fraser Rd EX8 23 E1
Freelands Cl EX8 23 E2
Frewins EX9 25 C2
Friars Gate EX2 3 C5
Friars Walk EX2 3 D5
Friernhay St EX4 3 B4
Frobisher Rd EX8 24 B4
Frog La EX5 13 H4
Frog St EX1 3 B5
Fulford Rd EX1 6 B5
Fulford Way EX5 27 C2
Fullers Ct EX2 3 B6
Furze Rd EX5 27 B2

Gabriel Ct EX2 3 C6
Gabriel Ho EX1 3 C5
Gabriels Wharf EX2 11 G4
Galahad Cl EX4 6 B3
Galmpton Rise EX4 6 A3
Gandy St EX4 3 C3
Garden Cl EX2 12 D3
Garden Ct EX9 25 E3
Gareth Cres EX4 6 B3
Garland Cl EX4 4 B4
Garratt Cl EX8 24 B3
Gater La EX1 3 C5
Generals Cl EX6 26 C3
Generals La EX6 26 C3
Geneva Cl EX2 12 A3
George St, Exeter EX1 3 C4
George St, Exmouth EX8 22 C4
Georges Cl EX1 6 C6
Gervase Av EX2 3 B6
Gibraltar Rd EX8 21 D5
Gibson Cl EX8 23 F1
Gilbert Av EX2 12 D3
Gilbrook EX5 27 B3
Gipsy Hill La EX1 7 F5
Gipsy Hill Mews EX1 7 G5
Gipsy La, Exeter EX1 7 G5
Gipsy La, Exmouth EX8 22 C2
Gissons EX6 18 A5
Gittisham Cl EX1 13 E1
Gladstone Rd EX1 11 H1
Glasshouse La EX2 17 H1
Glastonbury Cl EX4 6 B3
Glave Saunders Av EX2 12 D3
Glebe Cl, Exmouth EX8 23 G3

Glebe Cl, Lympstone EX8 21 D5
Glebelands, Exeter EX6 17 H5
Glebelands, Exmouth EX8 21 D5
Glen Cl EX5 14 C4
Glen Walk EX4 5 H3
Glenmore Rd EX2 12 B2
Glenthorne Rd EX4 4 D3
Glenwood Rise EX2 11 G3
Globe Hill EX5 27 B2
Globe La EX3 18 D4
Globefields EX3 18 D4
Gloucester Rd, Exeter EX4 4 B6
Gloucester Rd, Exmouth EX8 24 D3
Goldsmith St, Exeter EX4 3 C4
Goldsmith St, Wonford EX1 12 A1
Good Shepherd Dr EX2 3 D5
Gordon Rd, Exeter EX1 5 H6
Gordon Rd, Topsham EX3 18 C3
Gordons Pl EX2 12 B2
Gore La EX8 23 F5
Gorfin Cl EX8 23 F2
Gorse La EX8 24 C3
Govetts EX5 27 C2
Grace Rd EX2 11 F5
Gracey Ct EX5 9 B1
Grafton Rd EX4 4 D4
Grainger Cl EX2 12 D2
Granary La EX9 25 F2
Grandisson Ct EX2 12 B5
Grange Av EX8 22 C2
Grange Cl, Exmouth EX8 22 C2
Grange Cl, Lympstone EX8 21 E5
Grasslands Dr EX1 7 F4
Great Hill Vw EX4 5 H2
Greatwood Ter EX3 18 D3
Grecian Way EX2 12 D3
Green Cl EX8 22 D2
Green La, Exeter EX4 10 C2
Green La, Topsham EX3 19 G6
Green Mews EX9 25 D3
Green Tree Rd EX5 9 C2
Green Vw EX9 25 D3
Greenacres EX4 4 D2
Greenford Villas EX2 11 F3
Greenhaven EX9 25 C2
Greenhill Av, Exmouth EX8 22 D4
Greenhill Av, Lympstone EX8 21 D6
Greenpark Av EX1 7 E6
Greenpark Rd EX8 24 C4
Greenway, Exeter EX2 10 C3
Greenway, Woodbury EX5 27 B2
Greenway La EX9 25 D2
Greenwood Dr EX2 13 E2
Grenadier Rd EX1 7 F6
Grendon Rd EX1 11 H1
Grenville Av EX4 7 E4
Grenville Rd EX8 24 B4
Grindle Way EX5 14 A5
Grosvenor Pl EX1 5 H6
Grove Hill EX3 19 E3
Guildford Cl EX4 4 B6
Guinea St EX1 3 C5
Guinevere Way EX4 6 B4
Guinness La EX4 4 C5
Gussiford La EX8 22 C4
Guys Rd EX4 10 D1

Haccombe Cl EX4 10 C1
Hadrian Dr EX4 10 B1
Hadrians Way EX8 23 F2
Haldon Cl EX3 18 C3
Haldon Ct EX8 22 C1
Haldon Rd EX4 3 B3
Haldon View Ter EX2 12 A2
Haley Rd EX8 24 B4
Halsdon Av EX8 22 B2
Halsdon La EX8 22 B1
Halsdon Rd EX8 22 B3
Halse Hill La EX9 25 C3
Halses Cl EX4 4 B5
Halyards EX3 18 D4
Hambeer La EX2 10 C4
Hamilton Av EX2 12 A4
Hamilton Dr EX2 13 E2
Hamilton Gro EX6 26 D3
Hamilton La EX8 22 D3
Hamilton Rd, Exeter EX3 18 C3
Hamilton Rd, Exmouth EX8 23 E3
Hamlin Gdns EX1 6 B6
Hamlin La EX1 6 B5
Hamlyns La EX4 4 C4

Hammond Croft Way EX2 16 C1
Hampden Pl EX2 3 B6
Hampshire Cl EX4 10 C3
Hampstead La EX3 19 F6
Hampton Bldgs EX4 5 H5
Hanover Cl EX1 12 A1
Hanover Ct EX2 16 D1
Hanover Rd EX1 6 A6
Harbour Ct EX8 22 A4
Hardy Rd EX2 13 E2
Harebell Copse EX4 4 B5
Harefield EX8 21 E6
Harefield Cl EX4 3 A1
Harefield Rd EX8 20 E4
Harrier Way EX2 13 F3
Harringcourt Rd EX4 7 F3
Harrington Dr EX4 7 F3
Harrington Gdns EX4 7 F3
Harrington La EX4 6 D3
Hartley Rd EX8 22 C5
Hartopp Rd EX8 22 B3
Harts Cl EX1 7 F4
Harts La EX1 7 E5
Harwood Cl EX8 23 E1
Hatherleigh Rd EX2 11 E5
Haven Cl EX2 11 F3
Haven Rd EX2 3 B6
Hawkins La EX11 15 C5
Hawthorn Gro EX8 23 F1
Hawthorn Rd EX2 12 A4
Hawthorn Way EX2 11 E6
Hayes Barton Ct EX4 3 A5
Hayes Cl EX9 25 D2
Hayes Orch EX5 27 C2
Hayne Cl EX4 6 C5
Haytor Dr EX4 4 C5
Hazel Rd EX2 12 B5
Hazeldene Gdns EX8 22 C2
Hazelmead Rd EX5 14 C5
Headingley Cl EX2 12 D3
Headland Cl EX1 6 D6
Headland Cres EX1 6 D6
Headon Gdns EX2 12 B6
Heard Av EX8 23 F2
Heath Barton EX4 6 D3
Heath Brook Mews EX4 6 D3
Heath Rd EX2 12 C2
Heather Cl EX1 6 C6
Heather Grange EX11 15 B5
Heatherdale EX8 22 D4
Heavitree Pk EX1 12 B2
Heavitree Rd EX1 11 G1
Hele Rd EX4 3 A2
Helena Pl EX8 22 C4
Hellings Gdns EX5 9 B1
Hellings Park La EX5 8 C1
Heneaton Sq EX2 18 A1
Henley Rd EX8 23 E3
Hennock Ct EX2 11 G6
Hennock Rd EX2 11 G5
Henrietta Rd EX8 22 C4
Hensleigh Dr EX2 11 H2
Herbert Rd EX1 6 A5
Hereford Cl EX8 24 C3
Hereford Rd EX4 4 B6
Heron EX2 13 F2
Heron Ct EX8 22 D5
Heron Rd, Exeter EX2 10 B3
Heron Rd, Sandy Gate EX2 13 F1
Herschell Rd EX4 5 H5
Hexworthy Av EX4 4 B5
Heywood Dr EX6 26 C1
High Bank EX11 15 B6
High Cft EX4 5 E3
High Mdws EX4 10 C2
High St, Budleigh Salterton EX9 25 D4
High St, Exeter EX4 3 C4
High St, Exmouth EX8 22 B4
High St, Ide EX2 10 B6
High St, Topsham EX3 18 D3
Highbury Pk EX8 22 B1
Highcliffe Cl EX8 21 C6
Highcliffe Ct EX8 21 C6
Highcross Rd EX4 3 D1
Higher Aboveway EX6 18 A6
Higher Barley Mount EX4 10 C1
Higher Bedlands EX9 25 C2
Higher Broad Oak Rd EX11 15 B6
Higher Hoopern La EX4 5 G3
Higher Kings Av EX4 5 G4
Higher Marley Rd EX8 24 C2
Higher Shapter Cl EX3 19 E5
Higher Shapter St EX3 19 E5
Higher Summerlands EX1 11 H1
Higher Wear Rd EX2 18 A2
Highfield EX3 18 D2
Highfield La EX8 22 C5
Highview Gdns EX8 22 D4
Hill Barton Cl EX1 6 D5

Hill Barton La EX1 6 D6
Hill Barton Rd EX1 6 D6
Hill Cl EX4 5 G4
Hill Crest EX6 17 H5
Hill Dr EX8 24 A3
Hill La EX1 6 C5
Hill Rise EX1 6 D5
Hillcrest Pk EX4 5 F3
Hillsborough Av EX4 3 D1
Hillside Av EX4 3 D1
Hillyfield Rd EX1 6 D6
Hoker Rd EX2 12 B2
Holland Rd, Exeter EX2 10 D3
Holland Rd, Exmouth EX8 23 E2
Holley Cl EX6 17 H5
Hollow La EX1 7 E5
Holloway St EX2 3 D5
Hollowpits Ct EX2 16 C1
Holly Cl EX5 9 B1
Holly Mount Cl EX8 24 B3
Holly Rd EX2 12 A4
Holly Walk EX8 24 C3
Holman Way EX3 18 D4
Holne Ct EX4 4 C5
Holne Rise EX2 12 C2
Homefield Rd EX1 12 A1
Honey La EX1 7 G3
Honey Park Rd EX9 25 E2
Honeylands Dr EX4 6 B5
Honeylands Way EX4 6 B5
Honeysuckle Ct EX4 4 B5
Honiton Rd, Clyst Honiton EX5 8 A5
Honiton Rd, Exeter EX1 12 C2
Hooker Cl EX9 25 C2
Hoopern Av EX4 5 G4
Hoopern La EX4 3 D1
Hoopern St EX4 3 C1
Hope Pl EX2 12 B2
Hope Rd EX2 12 B2
Horseguards EX4 3 C1
Hospital La EX1 7 E5
Howard Cl EX4 4 C5
Howell Rd EX4 3 A2
Hulham Rd EX8 22 C2
Hummingbird Cl EX1 7 F4
Humphries Pk EX8 23 F1
Hunton Cl EX8 21 D5
Hurst Av EX2 12 C2
Hutchings Mead EX1 7 G4
Hylands Cl EX11 15 B6
Hylton Gdns EX4 10 D1

Iddesleigh Rd EX4 5 H5
Ide La, Exeter EX2 10 D6
Ide La, Ide EX2 10 B4
Ilex Cl, Exeter EX4 6 C3
Ilex Cl, Shillingford St George EX2 16 A5
Imperial Rd EX8 22 B4
Imperial St EX4 10 C2

INDUSTRIAL & RETAIL:

Bishops Ct Quarry Trading Est EX2 13 F3
Bittern Ind Units EX2 13 F1
Chelsea Trading Est EX2 13 E1
City Ind Est EX2 3 C6
Dart Bsns Pk EX3 19 F4
Dart Farm Shopping Village EX3 19 F4
Dinan Way Trading Est EX8 23 G2
Exe Bridges Retail Pk EX4 3 B6
Exeter Airport Bsns Pk EX6 9 B3
Guildhall Shopping Centre EX4 3 C4
Harlequins Shopping Centre EX4 3 C3
Heron Ind Units EX2 13 F2
Hungry Fox Est EX5 8 D2
Liverton Bsns Pk EX8 23 G1
Marsh Barton Trading Est EX2 11 F5
Matford Bsns Pk EX2 11 F6
Matford Pk EX2 17 E1
Merlin Bsns Pk EX6 9 B3
Park Five Bsns Centre EX2 13 F3
Pinhoe Trading Est EX4 7 E4
Pound La Ind Est EX8 22 D2
Sandpiper Ct Trading Est EX4 7 E3
Sowton Ind Est EX2 13 F2
Stone La Retail Pk EX2 11 E4
Swan Units EX2 13 F2
The Exeter Bsns Pk EX1 7 F6

Ingleside Ct EX9 25 D3
Inner Ting Tong EX9 25 A1
Iolanthe Dr EX4 6 B3
Iona Av EX8 22 C1
Iris Av EX2 11 E3
Iron Bri EX4 3 B3
Isca Rd, Exeter EX2 3 B6
Isca Rd, Exmouth EX8 22 D5
Isleworth Rd EX4 10 C2
Iveagh Ct EX4 4 C5
Ivy Cl EX2 12 C3
Ivydale EX8 24 C4

James Ct EX1 11 F2
Jardine Pk EX2 11 F5
Jarvis Cl EX8 23 F3
Jennifer Cl EX2 11 H3
Jesmond Rd EX1 5 H6
Jesmond Villas EX1 5 H6
Jocelyn Rd EX9 25 D2
John Levers Way EX4 10 D1
John St EX1 3 C5
Jubilee Cl EX6 17 H5
Jubilee Dr EX8 24 B4
Jubilee Gro EX8 21 E6
Jubilee Rd EX1 6 A5
Juniper Cl EX4 6 C3
Jupes Cl EX6 18 A6

Kalendarhay EX1 11 F1
Kalendarhay La EX1 3 C4
Kay Cl EX8 22 D2
Keats Cl EX8 24 B3
Kenbury Cres EX6 26 D4
Kenbury Dr EX2 16 D1
Kendall Cl EX4 5 H6
Kennerley Av EX4 6 C5
Kennford Rd EX2 11 F4
Kent Cl EX2 12 B2
Kersbrook La EX9 25 D1
Kerswill Rd EX4 10 C3
Kestor Dr EX4 4 B5
Kestrel Way EX2 13 F2
Keverel Rd EX8 22 C1
Kilbarran Rise EX4 5 E5
Kimberley Rd EX2 3 D5
Kincraig EX8 23 E4
King Arthurs Rd EX4 6 B3
King Edward St EX4 4 D4
King Henrys Rd EX2 12 A4
King St, Exeter EX1 3 B5
King St, Exmouth EX8 22 C4
King Stephen Cl EX4 3 C2
King William St EX4 3 D3
Kingdom Mews EX4 3 A2
Kingfisher Av EX2 10 B3
Kingfisher Ct EX4 7 E4
Kingfisher Dr EX4 5 G3
Kingfisher Way EX2 13 F1
Kings Rd EX4 6 A5
Kings Wharf EX2 3 C6
Kingsgate EX4 5 G5
Kingslake Rise EX8 22 B2
Kingsley Av EX4 6 C4
Kingston Rd EX8 23 E3
Kingsway EX2 12 A2
Kingswood Cl EX4 4 C5
Kinnerton Ct EX4 4 C5
Kinnerton Way EX4 4 B5
Kipling Cl EX8 24 B3
Kipling Dr EX2 12 B3
Knightley Rd EX2 11 H4
Knights Cres EX2 13 E3
Knowle Dr EX4 4 C6
Knowle Hill EX9 25 A3
Knowle Mews EX9 25 B2
Knowle Rd EX9 25 B2
Knowle Village EX9 25 B3

Laburnum Cl EX8 24 C3
Laburnum Rd EX2 12 A4
Lackaborough Ct EX2 16 B1
Ladysmith Rd EX1 6 A6
Lakelands Dr EX4 10 D1
Lakeside Av EX2 18 A1
Lamacraft Dr EX4 6 B5
Lamplough Rd EX8 21 F8
Lancaster Cl EX2 12 C2
Lancelot Rd EX4 6 B3
Landhayes Rd EX4 10 D1
Lands Rd EX4 7 E3
Landscore Rd EX4 10 D2
Langaton Gdns EX1 7 G4
Langaton La EX1 7 F3
Langerwehe Way EX8 22 A4
Langstone Dr EX8 22 D1
Lansdowne EX2 12 C3
Lansdowne Rd EX9 25 A3
Lansdowne Ter EX2 3 D6
Larch Cl EX8 24 C4
Larch Rd EX2 10 D4
Lark Cl EX4 5 G3
Larkbeare Rd EX2 3 D6
Latimer Rd EX4 6 B4
Laurel Rd EX2 12 A4
Laurel Rise EX8 23 E3
Lawn Rd EX8 22 C3
Lawrence Av EX4 10 D2
Lawrence Cres EX1 13 E1
Laxton Av EX1 12 D1
Leas Rd EX9 25 D3
Lebanon Cl EX4 5 H4
Legion Way EX2 11 E5
Leighdene Cl EX2 11 H3
Leighton Ter EX4 3 D2
Leslie Rd EX8 22 C3
Lestock Cl EX8 23 G3
Lethbridge Rd EX2 12 C2
Lewis Cres EX2 13 E4
Leypark Cl EX1 6 D6
Leypark Cres EX1 6 D6
Leypark Rd EX1 6 D6
Lichfield Rd EX4 4 B6
Lichgate Rd EX2 16 C1
Liffey Rise EX4 4 C5
Lilac Rd EX2 12 B4
Lily Mount EX4 4 B5
Lime Cl EX5 9 B2
Lime Gro, Exeter EX6 17 H4
Lime Gro, Exmouth EX8 24 B4
Lime Kiln La EX2 12 B6
Lime Tree Cl EX2 12 D4
Limegrove Rd EX4 10 D2
Limekiln La EX8 22 D5
Lincoln Cl EX8 24 D3
Lincoln Rd EX4 4 C6
Linda Cl EX1 12 D1
Linden Cl EX8 23 E1
Linden Vale EX4 3 B2
Linfield Gdns EX4 10 D2
Links Cl EX8 22 D3
Links Rd EX9 25 C4
Linnet Cl EX4 5 H2
Lisa Cl EX2 12 B2
Little Bicton Pl EX8 22 B4
Little Castle St EX4 3 D3
Little Johns Cross Hill EX2 10 C4
Little Knowle EX9 25 C3
Little Mdw EX8 24 D4
Little Queen St EX4 3 C4
Little Rack St EX1 3 C5
Little Silver EX4 3 B3
Little Silver La EX2 17 E4
Littledown Cl EX8 23 G3
Littleham Rd EX8 23 F3
Littlemead La EX8 21 F7
Littleway EX2 10 C3
Liverton Cl EX8 23 G2
Livery Dole Almhouses EX1 12 A1
Lloyds Cres EX1 6 D5
Lloyds Ct EX1 6 D5
Locarno Rd EX4 10 C2
Locksley Cl EX2 17 H1
Lodge Hill EX4 5 E5
London Inn Sq EX4 3 D3
Long Causeway EX8 22 C4
Long Copp EX9 25 E2
Long La EX8 22 D4
Long Mdw EX5 27 C2
Long Pk EX5 27 C1
Longacres EX2 11 H2
Longbrook La EX8 21 E6
Longbrook St EX4 3 D3
Longbrook Ter EX4 3 D3
Longdown Rd EX6 10 A4
Longfield Est EX6 26 C1
Longmeadow EX5 13 H4
Longmeadow Rd EX8 21 D6
Lonsdale Rd EX1 12 C1
Looe Rd EX4 3 A2
Loram Way EX2 16 D1
Lords Way EX2 12 D3
Louisa Pl EX8 22 C5
Louisa Ter EX8 22 B5
Lovelace Cres EX8 23 E2
Lovelace Gdns EX2 16 C1
Lovell Cl EX8 24 B4
Lovering Cl EX8 24 B3
Lower Albert St EX1 5 H6
Lower Argyll Rd EX4 4 D3
Lower Av EX1 6 A6
Lower Broad Oak Rd EX11 15 C6
Lower Coombe St EX1 3 C5
Lower Duck St EX6 18 A6
Lower Harrington La EX4 7 F4
Lower Hill Barton Rd EX1 12 D1
Lower Kings Av EX4 5 G4
Lower La EX3 19 G5
Lower North St EX4 3 B3
Lower St Germans Rd EX4 3 D1
Lower Shapter St EX3 19 E5
Lower Summerlands EX1 11 H1
Lower Wear Rd EX2 17 H1
Lucas Av EX4 5 H5
Lucky La EX2 3 C5
Ludwell La EX2 12 B3
Lustleigh Cl EX2 11 G6
Lymeborne Av EX1 12 B1
Lyncombe Cl EX4 5 H4
Lyndhurst Rd, Exeter EX2 11 H2
Lyndhurst Rd, Exmouth EX8 22 C2
Lynwood Av EX4 3 A5

Madagascar Cl EX8 23 F2
Maddocks Row EX4 3 C4
Madeira Ct EX8 22 C5
Madeira Villas EX8 22 C3
Madeira Walk EX9 25 E4
Madison Av EX1 6 C6
Maer Bay Ct EX8 22 D5
Maer La EX8 22 D6
Maer Rd EX8 22 D5
Maer Vale EX8 22 D5
Magdalen Cotts EX1 11 G1
Magdalen Gdns EX2 11 H2
Magdalen Rd EX2 11 G2
Magdalen St EX2 3 D5
Magnolia Av, Exeter EX2 12 B3
Magnolia Av, Exmouth EX8 23 F3
Magpie Cres EX2 10 B3
Main Rd, Exeter EX4 7 F4
Main Rd, Exminster EX6 17 G3
Majorfield Rd EX3 18 D4
Mallard Rd EX2 13 F2
Mallison Cl EX4 4 C5
Malt Field EX8 21 E6
Malvern Gdns EX2 12 B3
Mamhead Rd EX2 12 D3
Mamhead Vw EX8 22 A5
Manaton Cl EX2 16 D1
Manaton Ct EX2 16 D1
Manchester Rd EX8 22 B4
Manchester St EX8 22 B4
Mandrake Cl EX2 11 E5
Mandrake Rd EX2 11 E6
Manor Pk EX5 13 H4
Mansfield Rd EX4 5 H5
Mansfield Ter EX9 25 E2
Manston Rd EX1 6 A6
Manston Ter EX2 12 A1
Manstree Rd EX2 16 A4
Maple Dr EX8 24 C3
Maple Rd, Broadclyst EX5 9 B2
Maple Rd, Exeter EX4 10 D2
Marcom Cl EX8 24 C3
Marcus Rd EX8 23 E1
Mardon Hill EX4 5 E4
Margaret Rd EX4 6 A4
Marina Ct EX8 22 D5
Marine Ct EX9 25 E4
Marine Par EX9 25 E4
Marine Way EX8 22 B4
Marions Way EX8 24 C4
Maristow Av EX8 22 C1
Maritime Ct EX2 11 F3
Market St, Exeter EX1 3 C4
Market St, Exmouth EX8 22 B4
Markham La EX2 16 A1
Marlborough Cl EX8 24 D4
Marlborough Ct, Lyndhurst Rd, Exeter EX2 11 H2
Marlborough Ct, Matford Bsns Pk, Exeter EX2 16 D1
Marlborough Dr EX2 13 E2
Marlborough Rd EX2 11 H2
Marley Dr EX8 24 C1
Marley Rd, Exmouth EX8 24 A4
Marley Rd, Exmouth EX8 24 C3
Marpool Cres EX8 22 D3
Marpool Hill EX8 22 C3
Marsh Barton Rd EX2 11 E4
Marsh Green Rd EX2 11 F4
Marsh La EX3 19 F3
Martins La EX1 3 C4
Martins Rd EX8 24 D4
Marwood Rd EX6 9 B3
Mary Arches St EX4 3 B4
Maryfield Av EX4 5 G4
Marypole Rd EX4 6 A4
Marypole Walk EX4 6 A4
Masefield Rd EX4 6 D4
Masey Rd EX8 23 E2
Matford Av EX2 11 H2
Matford La EX2 11 G3
Matford Park Rd EX2 11 G6
Matford Rd EX2 11 H2
Matthews Ct EX4 7 E3
May St EX4 5 H5
Mayfield Dr EX8 23 E5
Mayfield Rd, Exeter EX2 12 B2
Mayfield Rd, Pinhoe EX4 7 F4
Mayflower Av EX4 5 G2
Mead Cotts EX8 23 G4
Meadow Cl, Budleigh Salterton EX9 25 D3
Meadow Cl, Exeter EX5 14 C4
Meadow Cl, Exmouth EX8 21 E6
Meadow Rd EX9 25 D4
Meadow St EX8 22 C4
Meadow View Rd EX8 23 F1
Meadow Way EX2 12 A2
Meadowbrook Cl EX4 4 B5
Meeting La EX8 21 D5
Meeting St EX8 22 C4
Meetways La EX8 23 E5
Melbourne Pl EX2 3 D6
Melbourne St EX2 3 D6
Meldon Ct EX9 25 E3
Membury Cl EX1 13 E1
Mercer Ct EX2 12 B5
Meresyke EX8 23 E4
Merlin Cres EX4 6 B3
Mermaid Yd EX1 3 C5
Merrion Av EX8 23 E4
Merrivale Rd EX4 10 C3
Michigan Way EX4 5 G2
Middlewood Hill EX6 26 C5
Midway EX8 23 F3
Midway Ter EX2 11 E6
Milbury Cl EX6 17 H4
Milbury La EX6 17 H5
Mildmay Cl EX4 4 D6
Mile Gdns EX4 6 B3
Mile La EX4 6 B4
Milestones Cotts EX6 17 H6
Mill La, Clyst Honiton EX5 8 B4
Mill La, Countess Wear EX2 12 B6
Mill La, Exeter EX2 11 E6
Mill La, Exton EX3 20 B1
Mill Rd EX2 12 B6
Mill Yard EX2 12 A6
Millbrook La EX2 12 A5
Miller Cl EX2 12 D3
Miller Way EX6 17 G4
Milletts Cl EX6 17 H5
Millside EX2 11 G3
Milton Cl EX8 24 B3
Milton Rd EX2 12 A4
Mimosa Ct EX9 25 F3
Mincinglake Rd EX4 6 A4
Minster Rd EX6 17 H4
Mirey La EX5 27 B2
Mission Ct EX4 3 B5
Mitre La EX4 3 B4
Modred Cl EX4 6 B4
Monitor Cl EX2 11 F3
Monkerton Dr EX1 7 F4
Monks Rd EX4 6 A5
Monkswell Rd EX4 5 H5
Monmouth Av EX3 19 E4
Monmouth Hill EX3 18 D5
Monmouth St EX3 19 E5
Mont Le Grand EX1 12 A1
Mont Le Grand Rd EX1 12 A1
Montague Gdns EX9 25 B3
Montague Rise EX4 3 D2
Monterey Gdns EX4 5 H4
Montpelier Ct EX4 3 B2
Montpellier Ct EX8 22 C4
Montpellier Rd EX8 22 C4
Moon Ridge EX2 18 B2
Moonhill Cl EX2 16 D1
Moor La, Budleigh Salterton EX9 25 C2
Moor La, Exeter EX2 13 F1
Moorfield Cl EX8 22 D2
Moorfield Rd EX8 22 D2
Moorhaven EX9 25 D2
Moorhaven Rd EX9 25 B3
Moorland Way EX4 4 C5
Moorlands EX11 15 B3
Moormead EX9 25 C3
Moorpark EX8 23 E5
Moorview Cl EX4 5 H4
Morley Rd EX4 6 A5
Mortimer Ct EX2 12 B5
Morton Cres EX8 22 A5
Morton Cres Mews EX8 22 B5
Morton Rd EX8 22 B4
Morven Dr EX8 22 C1
Mosshayne La EX1 7 H2
Mount Howe EX3 19 E5
Mount Pleasant Rd EX4 5 H5
Mount Pleasent Av EX8 24 A4
Mount Radford Cres EX2 11 G2
Mount Wear Sq EX2 18 A1
Mountain Cl EX8 23 G2
Mountbatten Cl EX8 23 E1
Mowbray Av EX4 3 D2
Mudbank La EX8 22 B2
Mulberry Cl EX1 6 D6
Musgrave Row EX4 3 C3
Mutton La EX2 16
Myrtle Cl EX2 11
Myrtle Rd EX4 10
Myrtle Row EX8 22

Nadder Park Rd EX4 10
Napier Ter EX4 3
Nasmith Cl EX8 23
Needlewood Cl EX11 15
Nelson Cl EX3 18
Nelson Dr EX8 23
Nelson Rd EX4 3
Nelson Way EX2 13
Neptune Ct EX1 3
New Bldgs, Broadclyst EX5 9
New Bldgs, Exeter EX4 3
New Bridge St EX4 3
New North Rd, Exeter EX4 3
New North Rd, Exmouth EX8 22
New Rd, Exeter EX6 26
New Rd, Ottery St Mary EX11 15
New St EX8 22
New Valley Rd EX4 4
Newcombe Gdns EX1 12
Newcombe St EX1 12
Newcourt Rd EX2 18
Newfoundland Cl EX4 5
Newhayes Cl EX2 10
Newlands Av EX8 23
Newlands Cl EX2 10
Newman Ct EX4 10
Newman Rd EX4 10
Newport Rd EX2 18
Newtown Cl EX1 5
Nicholas Rd EX1 12
Nightingale Walk EX2 10
Norman Cl EX8 24
Normandy Cl EX8 23
Normandy Rd EX1 12
North Av EX1 6
North Bridge Pl EX4 3
North Gate Ct EX4 3
North Lawn Ct EX1 12
North Park Rd EX4 5
North St, Exeter EX4 3
North St, Exeter EX3 19
North St, Exmouth EX8 22
North St, Wonford EX1 12
Northernhay Gate EX4 3
Northernhay Pl EX4 3
Northernhay Sq EX4 3
Northernhay St EX4 3
Northview Rd EX9 25
Norwich Cl EX8 24
Norwich Rd EX4 4
Norwood Av EX2 11
Nurseries Cl, Exton EX3 20
Nurseries Cl, Topsham EX3 18
Nursery Cl EX8 22
Nursery Mews EX8 22
Nutbrook EX8 22
Nutwell Rd EX8 21

Oak Cl, Exminster EX6 17
Oak Cl, Pinhoe EX1 7
Oak Cl, Shillingford Abbot EX2 16
Oak Rd, Exeter EX4 10
Oak Rd, Ottery St Mary EX11 15
Oak Ridge EX2 16
Oak Tree Cl EX5 9
Oakfield Rd EX4 3
Oakfield St EX1 12
Oakhayes Rd EX5 27
Oakleigh Rd EX8 22
Oakley Cl EX1 7
Oaktree Cl EX8 24
Oaktree Pl EX2 16
Oakwood Rise EX8 24
Oberon Rd EX1 7
Oil Mill La EX5 14
Okehampton Pl EX4 3
Okehampton Rd EX4 3
Okehampton St EX4 3
Okewood Ct EX8 22
Old Abbey Ct EX2 11
Old Bakery Cl EX4 4
Old Bystock Dr EX8 24
Old Coach Rd EX5 9
Old Dawlish Rd EX6 16
Old Ebford La EX3 19
Old Ide La EX2 10
Old Market Cl EX2 11
Old Matford La EX2 17
Old Mill Cl EX2 11
Old Park Rd EX4 3
Old Pavilion Cl EX2 12
Old Pinn La EX1 7
Old Rydon Cl EX2 13

Spruce Cl, Exmouth EX8 24 C3
Spurway Hill EX6 17 G6
Spyders La EX8 24 B4
Staddon Cl EX4 6 C6
Stafford Rd EX4 10 D2
Stanford Rd EX2 12 D2
Stanley Mews EX9 25 D3
Stanley Sq EX3 18 D4
Stanley Walk EX8 24 D3
Stanwey EX1 12 B1
Staplake La EX6 26 B3
Staplake Rd EX6 26 C1
Staplake Rise EX6 26 C1
Star Barton La EX4 4 A1
Station Rd, Broadclyst EX5 9 B3
Station Rd, Budleigh Salterton EX9 25 D3
Station Rd, Clyst Honiton EX5 8 C1
Station Rd, Exeter EX4 3 A1
Station Rd, Exminster EX6 18 A6
Station Rd, Exton EX3 20 B2
Station Rd, Ide EX2 10 B6
Station Rd, Pinhoe EX1 7 F3
Station Rd, Topsham EX3 18 D4
Station Yd EX4 3 B3
Steeple Dr EX2 16 C1
Stepcote Hill EX1 3 B5
Steps Cl EX1 7 F4
Stevenstone Rd EX8 23 E3
Stewart Cl EX8 23 F2
Stirling Ho EX1 3 D4
Stocker Rd EX4 5 E4
Stoke Hill EX4 5 H4
Stoke Hill Cres EX4 5 H4
Stoke Meadow Cl EX4 5 H3
Stoke Rd EX4 4 D1
Stoke Valley Rd EX4 5 G2
Stokes Mead EX5 27 C1
Stone La EX8 21 D6
Stoneborough Ct EX9 25 E3
Stoneborough La EX9 25 E3
Stoneyford Pk EX9 25 E3
Stony La EX8 20 E3
Stover Ct EX1 5 G6
Strand EX8 22 B4
Strand Ct EX3 18 D5
Strand Vw EX3 19 E5
Stratford Av EX4 7 E4
Strawberry Av EX2 16 D1
Strawberry Hill EX8 21 D6
Stream Ct EX2 3 C6
Streatham Dr EX4 3 B1
Streatham Rise EX4 3 B1
Stuart Rd EX1 12 B1
Sturges Rd EX8 23 F2
Sullivan Rd EX2 12 D2
Summer Cl, Exeter EX4 6 C5
Summer Cl, Exmouth EX8 23 F3
Summer La, Exeter EX4 6 C3
Summer La, Exmouth EX8 21 F7
Summerfield EX5 27 C1
Summerland St EX1 5 G6
Summerway EX4 6 C5
Sunhill Av EX3 18 D3
Sunhill La EX3 18 D3
Sunnyfield EX5 9 B1
Sunnymoor Cl EX1 7 G3
Sunwine Pl EX8 22 C5
Surbiton Cres EX4 10 C3
Sussex Cl EX4 10 B3
Swains Ct EX3 18 D4
Swains Rd EX9 25 F2
Swallow Ct EX4 4 D4
Swallow Dr EX2 10 B3
Swallowfield Rd EX2 12 C5
Swan Ct EX2 11 G3
Swan Rd EX6 26 C2
Swan Yd EX4 3 B6
Sweetbrier La EX1 6 B6
Swiss Cl EX8 24 A3
Sycamore Cl, Broadclyst EX5 9 B2
Sycamore Cl, Exeter EX1 12 C2
Sycamore Cl, Exmouth EX8 23 F1
Sydney Rd EX2 11 E3
Sylvan Av EX4 5 H4
Sylvan Cl EX8 21 F8
Sylvan Rd EX4 5 H4
Sylvania Dr EX4 5 H2

Taddiforde Rd EX4 3 A1
Taddyforde Ct EX4 3 A1
Taddyforde Est EX4 3 A1
Tamarisk Cl EX4 6 C2
Tan La EX2 11 F3
Tappers Cl EX3 18 D3
Taps Cl EX6 17 H5
Tarbet Av EX1 6 B5
Taunton Cl EX2 11 E4
Tavistock Rd EX4 3 A2
Teazle Ct EX2 3 C6
Tedburn Rd EX4 10 A2
Tedstone La EX8 21 F5
Tedstone Rd EX8 20 F4
Telegraph La EX11 15 A2
Telford Rd EX4 3 A2
Temple Rd EX2 3 D5
Tennyson Av EX2 12 A4
Tennyson Way EX8 24 B3
Thackeray Rd EX4 6 D5
The Arch EX5 27 B2
The Avenue EX3 20 B2
The Beacon EX8 22 B5
The Broadway EX8 23 F3
The College EX2 10 B5
The Copse, Exeter EX2 18 B2
The Copse, Exmouth EX8 24 D4
The Crescent EX8 23 F3
The Fairway EX4 5 H3
The Green, Exeter EX2 10 B5
The Green, Exmouth EX8 23 G3
The Hams EX2 10 B5
The Hollows EX8 22 C3
The Lawn EX9 25 D4
The Maltings EX2 12 A1
The Marles EX8 22 D1
The Mede, Exeter EX4 6 D5
The Mede, Topsham EX3 18 D4
The Mint EX4 3 B4
The Panney EX4 6 B5
The Poplars EX4 7 F3
The Quarries EX4 10 B3
The Quay EX2 3 C6
The Queens Dr EX4 5 E4
The Retreat Dr EX3 18 C2
The Ridings EX3 19 G4
The Rolle EX9 25 E4
The Rosemullion EX9 25 D4
The Royal Av EX8 22 B4
The Shrubbery EX3 18 D4
The Square EX4 4 D5
The Strand, Exmouth EX8 22 B4
The Strand, Lympstone EX8 21 C6
The Strand, Starcross EX6 26 C1
The Strand, Topsham EX3 18 D5
The Triangles EX1 11 G1
The Village EX5 13 H4
The Wicket EX2 12 D3
Third Av, Exeter EX2 13 E1
Third Av, Lower Wear EX2 18 B2
Third Av, Polsloe EX1 6 A6
Thomas Cl, Bystock EX8 24 B3
Thomas Cl, Exmouth EX8 23 F6
Thomas La EX4 3 A1
Thompson Rd EX1 6 B5
Thorn Cl EX1 12 C1
Thornberry Av EX1 12 C1
Thorndale Cts EX4 4 B4
Thornfield Cl EX8 21 F8
Thornpark Rise EX1 6 C6
Thornton Hill EX4 3 D1
Thorpe Av EX8 24 A3
Three Corner Pl EX2 16 D1
Thurlow Rd EX4 5 H5
Tidwell Cl EX9 25 D2
Tidwell La EX9 25 E1
Tidwell Rd EX9 25 D2
Tin La EX2 10 D3
Tintagel Cl EX4 6 B3
Tipton La EX11 15 C1
Tithebarn Copse EX1 7 G4
Tithebarn La EX1 7 F5
Toadpit La EX11 15 C2
Tollards Rd EX2 12 B5
Topsham Rd EX2 3 D6
Tor Cl EX4 6 B4
Toronto Rd EX4 5 H5
Tottons Ct EX2 16 C1
Tower St EX8 22 B4
Tower Vw EX5 9 B3
Tower Walk EX2 16 D1
Towerfield EX3 18 D2
Town End EX5 9 B1
Town Hill EX5 9 B1
Town La EX5 27 C2
Townfield EX6 17 H5
Towsington La EX6 17 G6
Trafalgar Pl EX4 5 G5
Trafalgar Rd EX8 21 D5
Trafford Mews EX2 12 D3
Travershes Cl EX8 22 D1
Trefusis Pl EX8 22 C5
Trefusis Ter EX8 22 C5
Trelivan Cl EX8 24 D3
Tremford Ct EX9 25 C3
Trentbridge Sq EX2 12 D3
Tresillian Cotts EX3 19 E6
Tresillian Gdns, Exeter EX4 5 H5
Tresillian Gdns, Topsham EX3 19 E5
Trews Weir Reach EX2 11 G3
Trinfield Av EX8 22 C1
Trinity Ct EX1 3 D4
Tristan Cl EX4 6 B3
Trood La EX2 17 E3
Truro Dr, Exeter EX4 4 C6
Truro Dr, Exmouth EX8 24 C3
Trusham Rd EX2 11 F4
Tuckfield Cl EX2 12 B3
Tudor Ct EX4 3 B5
Tudor St EX4 3 B5
Tuffery Ct EX4 6 A5
Tugela Ter EX5 13 H4
Turner Av EX8 22 D4
Two Acre Ct EX2 16 B1

Underhill EX8 21 C6
Underhill Cl EX8 21 D6
Underhill Cres EX8 21 D6
Underhill Ter EX3 18 D4
Union Rd EX4 5 G5
Union St, Exeter EX2 3 A6
Union St, Exmouth EX8 22 C4
Uplands Dr EX4 6 B4
Upper Church St EX8 22 C4
Upper Paul St EX4 3 C3
Upper Stoneborough La EX9 25 D3
Upper West Ter EX9 25 D3

Vachell Cres EX2 13 E1
Vale Rd EX8 23 E3
Vales Rd EX9 25 F3
Valley Park Cl EX4 5 G2
Valley Rd, Clyst St Mary EX5 14 C4
Valley Rd, Exeter EX4 4 D5
Valley Way EX8 24 D3
Vansittart Dr EX8 24 B4
Varco Sq EX2 12 D3
Vaughan Rd EX1 6 C6
Vaughan Rise EX1 6 C6
Veitch Gdns EX2 16 C1
Velwell Rd EX4 3 B2
Venny Bri EX4 7 E4
Verney St EX1 5 G6
Vernon Rd EX8 24 C4
Vestry Dr EX2 16 C1
Vicarage Gdns EX2 10 D3
Vicarage La EX4 7 F2
Vicarage Rd EX6 26 C4
Victor Cl EX1 12 B1
Victor La EX1 12 B1
Victor St EX1 12 B1
Victoria Park Rd EX2 11 H2
Victoria Pl, Budleigh Salterton EX9 25 D4
Victoria Pl, Exmouth EX8 22 C4
Victoria Rd, Exeter EX4 5 G5
Victoria Rd, Exmouth EX8 22 A5
Victoria Rd, Topsham EX3 18 D4
Victoria St EX4 5 G5
Victoria Way EX8 22 A4
Victoria Yard EX4 3 C3
Village Cl EX8 23 G3
Vine Cl EX2 11 G2
Vine Ho EX9 25 E3
Vision Hill Rd EX9 25 E2
Vuefield Hill EX2 10 C4

Wade Cl EX8 23 F2
Waggoners Way EX4 4 D5
Wallace Av EX4 6 C5
Walls Cl EX8 24 C4
Walnut Cl EX6 17 H5
Walnut Gdns EX4 3 A2
Walnut Gro EX8 23 E4
Walnut Rd EX2 12 B4
Walpole Cl EX4 6 D4
Walton Rd EX2 12 D2
Wardrew Rd EX4 10 D2
Warneford Gdns EX8 24 D4
Warren Cl EX11 15 B5
Warren Dr EX9 25 F2
Warren La EX4 3 D2
Warren Pk EX11 15 B4
Warwick Av EX1 12 D1
Warwick Rd EX1 12 D1
Warwick Way EX4 6 D4
Water La EX2 3 C6
Waterbeer St EX4 3 C4
Watergate EX2 3 C5
Waterloo Rd EX2 11 E4
Waterside EX2 3 C6
Waterslade La EX5 8 C5
Watery La EX5 27 B1
Waverley Av EX4 3 D2
Waverley Rd EX8 22 C2
Waybrook Cres EX2 11 F6
Waybrook La EX2 16 B3
Wayland Av EX2 11 G2
Wayside Cres EX1 6 C6
Wear Barton Rd EX2 18 A1
Wear Cl EX2 18 A2
Weavers Ct EX2 3 C6
Webley Rd EX2 10 D4
Weirfield Rd EX2 3 D6
Welcome St EX2 11 F3
Well Oak Pk EX2 12 A3
Well St, Exeter EX4 5 G6
Well St, Starcross EX6 26 D2
Wellington Cl EX2 13 E1
Wellington Rd EX2 11 E4
Wellpark Cl EX4 10 C1
Wells Cl EX8 24 D3
Wellswood Gdns EX4 10 C2
Wendover Way EX2 12 C5
Wentworth Gdns EX4 10 C3
Wesley Cl EX2 11 E4
Wesley Way EX2 16 C1
Wessex Cl EX3 18 C3
West Av EX4 3 D1
West Clyst Rd EX1 7 G2
West Down La EX8 23 H4
West Garth Rd EX4 4 D2
West Grove Rd EX2 11 G2
West Hill EX9 25 C4
West Hill Ct EX9 25 C4
West Hill Gdns EX9 25 C4
West Hill La, Budleigh Salterton EX9 25 C3
West Hill La, Ottery St Mary EX11 15 C3
West Hill Rd EX11 15 A5
West St EX1 3 B5
West Ter EX9 25 D3
West View Ter EX4 3 B4
Westbourne Ter EX9 25 D4
Westbrook Cl EX4 6 C5
Westcombe EX2 16 C1
Western Dr EX6 26 D2
Western Rd EX4 3 A4
Western Way, Exeter EX1 3 C5
Western Way, Exeter EX1 11 G1
Westfield EX6 18 A6
Westfield Cl EX9 25 D3
Westfield Rd EX9 25 D3
Westlands EX8 23 E5
Westminster Cl EX8 24 D3
Westminster Rd EX4 4 B6
Westown Rd EX2 10 A6
Westward Dr EX8 22 C4
Westwood Hill EX6 26 C4
Westwood La EX6 10 A3
Weycroft Cl EX1 13 E1
Wheatley Cl EX4 10 B2
Wheatley Ct EX1 3 C5
Wheatsheaf Way EX2 11 E6
Whiddon La EX2 10 A6
Whipton Barton Rd EX1 6 C5
Whipton La EX1 12 B1
Whipton Rd EX4 6 B5
Whipton Village Rd EX4 6 C5
Whitchurch Av EX2 12 C3
White Cross Rd EX5 27 C1
White Farm La EX11 15
White St EX3 18
White Stones EX8 22
Whitebeam Cl EX4 6
Whitehall La EX3 18
Whiteside Cl EX2 12
Whitethorn Pk EX4 5
Whiteway Dr EX1 12
Whitlow Copse EX2 12
Whitman Cl EX8 24
Whitycombe Way EX4 4
Widecombe Way EX4 5
Widgery Rd EX4 6
Wilcocks Rd EX4 7
Wilford Rd EX2 12
Willeys Av EX2 11
Williams Av EX2 3
Willoughby Cl EX8 24
Willow Av EX8 24
Willow Ct EX2 12
Willow Gdns EX5 9
Willow Walk EX4 5
Willsdown Rd EX2 16
Wilmot Cl EX8 23
Wilthshire Cl EX4 10
Wilton Way EX1 13
Wiltshier Cl EX5 9
Winchester Av EX4 4
Winchester Dr EX8 24
Windermere Cl EX4 10
Windmill La EX11 15
Windsor Cl EX4 3
Windsor Sq EX8 22
Winkleigh Cl EX2 11
Winslade Park Av EX5 13
Winston Rd EX8 24
Withycombe Park Dr EX8 24
Withycombe Rd EX8 22
Withycombe Village Rd EX8 22
Wonford Rd EX2 11
Wonford St EX2 12
Woodah Rd EX4 10
Woodbine Ter EX4 3
Woodbury Ct EX8 22
Woodbury Rd, Clyst St George EX3 19
Woodbury Rd, Exeter EX5 27
Woodbury Rd, Exeter EX5 27
Woodbury Rd, Exmouth EX8 20
Woodbury Vw, Broadclyst EX5 9
Woodbury Vw, Exeter EX2 10
Woodfield Cl EX8 23
Woodland Mews EX5 9
Woodland Rd, Broadclyst EX5 9
Woodland Rd, Exeter EX1 7
Woodlands EX9 25
Woodlands Dr EX8 24
Woodlands Way EX5 14
Woodleigh Cl EX4 5
Woodstock Rd EX2 12
Woodville Rd, Exeter EX2 11
Woodville Rd, Exmouth EX8 22
Woodwater La, Exeter EX2 12
Woodwater La, Exeter EX2 12 D
Woolaway Av EX6 18 A
Woolsery Av EX4 6 C
Woolsery Cl EX4 6 C
Woolsery Gro EX4 6 C
Wordsworth Cl EX8 24 E
Wotton La EX8 21 E
Wrefords Cl EX4 4 D
Wrefords Dr EX4 4 D
Wrefords La EX4 4 D
Wrights La EX8 24 E
Wykes Rd EX1 6 A
Wynards La EX2 3 D
Wyndham Av EX1 12 A
Wynford Rd EX4 6 A

Yeoford Way EX2 17 E
Yew Tree Cl, Exeter EX4 5 H
Yew Tree Cl, Exmouth EX8 24 E
York Cl EX8 23 F
York Rd EX4 3 D
York Ter EX4 5 G

Edition 361 G 03.0